Mirror, Mirror

by Sarah Treem

A SAMUEL FRENCH ACTING EDITION

FOUNDED 1830

SAMUELFRENCH.COM

ISBN 978-0-573-69826-2   Printed in U.S.A.   #29622

MUSIC USE NOTE

**IMPORTANT BILLING AND CREDIT
REQUIREMENTS**

MIRROR MIRROR was first produced at the Yale School of Drama on November 11, 2005. The performance was directed by Nick Avila, with sets by Sara Clement, costumes by Mike Floyd, lighting by Bryan Keller, and sound by Sharath Patel, with dramaturgy by Rachel Rusch. The production stage manager was Adam Ganderson. The cast was as follows:

GRETCHEN	Corena Chase
HOYT	Richard Gallagher
ROY/ROSE	Blake Hackler
LAUREL	Bridget Jones
COSTEN	Jacob Knoll
BADGER	Allen Read
LIBBY	Alexis McGuinness
HONEY	Lauren Worsham
DONNIE	Alexander Rubin
RONNIE	Paul Spera

CHARACTERS

GRETCHEN BLACK – 17, Most popular girl in school.

BADGER BIERS – 17, Gretchen's boyfriend. Most popular boy in school. Captain of the football team.

COSTEN LYONS – 18, Badger's best friend. Richest boy in school.

LIBBY SUNDAY – 17, Gretchen's new best friend. Hoyt's ex-girlfriend. Valedictorian. On scholarship.

HOYT MONROE – 18, Tortured teenage artist. Libby's ex-boyfriend.

LAUREL BUCHANAN – 16, Hoyt's best friend. President of the drama club. Costen's second cousin.

HONEY – 15, Stage manager in the drama club. Nerd.

DONNIE – 17, Actor in the drama club. Ronnie's best friend.

RONNIE – 17 Actor in the drama club. Donnie's best friend.

ROSE WHITE – 16, New girl. This is a boy's part.

SETTING

A private high school in the South. A gym. An auditorium.
A bathroom. Boo-yeah.

TIME

Fall. Present day.

(AT RISE: An empty space. Cloudy. Liminal. The space before a story starts.)

*(A boy, **ROY**, 17, walks into the space. He's wearing a backpack and a baseball cap. He snaps his fingers.)*

(A mirror descends in front of him. Large and institutional.)

*(**ROY** looks at the audience. Smiles. He takes a make-up case out of his backpack and a long white dress the color of moonlight.)*

ROY. Mirrors are strange things. Sometimes they seem to have minds of their own. Especially when you're young. And you don't know what you're looking for.
I was young once upon a time. In a land not so far away.

*(**ROY** takes off his shirt.)*

Every autumn, as the summer sun finally relinquished her gentle throne to cold crown of winter, there was a tremendous celebration.

(He takes off his shoes.)

A ritual as old as the ancient land itself.

*(**ROY** takes off his pants.)*

A great ball.

*(**ROY** puts on the dress.)*

Princes and Princesses came from all over to attend.

*(**ROY** puts on a pair of heels.)*

The air tasted like honeysuckle and peach.

*(**ROY** puts on a wig of long black hair.)*

The earth itself trembled to be tread upon.

(ROY opens his make-up case and applies very red lipstick.)

ROY. *(cont.)* And they called it…Homecoming.

(He looks at himself in the mirror. He is stunning. He smiles.)

It's a long story.

(ROY snaps his fingers again. Down comes a door and toilet stalls. He's now inside a girls' high school bathroom.)

(A knock at the door.)

One second.

(The door swings open. GRETCHEN, 17, enters. She's all dressed up for the dance.)

GRETCHEN. Libby? Oh, I'm sorry. I was looking for my friend.

ROY. I was just leaving.

(ROY packs his clothes and make-up back into his backpack.)

GRETCHEN. I don't know you, do I?

ROY. I don't think so. I'm new.

GRETCHEN. What's your name?

ROY. Rose White. What's yours?

GRETCHEN. Gretchen Black.

(ROY, who will henceforth be known as ROSE, holds out her hand to shake. GRETCHEN just stares at her.)

GRETCHEN. I just had my nails done.

(A beat. Then ROSE smiles brightly.)

ROSE. They look sharp.

(ROSE exits.)

(GRETCHEN looks down, and takes a deep breath.)

GRETCHEN. Mirror Mirror on the wall, who's the fairest of them all?

(**GRETCHEN** *looks up suddenly. She gasps. Turns around. There's nobody there. She turns back to the mirror.*)

GRETCHEN. Don't you pull that shit with me. I will break you.

When I was a child I had a beautiful mirror. Gilded and very old. It was my great grandmother's mirror. Brought over from Vienna on a first class steamer. The mirror hung in the grand hallway. I cleaned it incessantly. Every time I passed it. The mirror loved me for that. And always made sure I looked beautiful in return. We were best friends. Until one day...

The mirror showed me something just *wicked*. Something that never should have been. I told my father, who banished the evildoer from the land.

But the poor mirror never recovered. It was traumatized. It stopped working properly. It reflected back all the wrong faces. It was a very sick mirror. It started infecting other mirrors. Soon the town was plagued with demented mirrors. The townspeople became afraid to use the bathrooms. I knew I had to do something. What do you supposed I did? I broke the mirror. Smashed it in, late one night, with the heel of my shoe. Then I picked up the shattered pieces of glass and sewed them into my skin. And from that day forth, I've carried them with me wherever I go. And everyone everywhere always asks me about my skin. They want to know what makes it shimmer so.

(**GRETCHEN** *looks down at her feet. She smirks at the mirror.*)

(*a threat*) What do you think of my shoes? Are the heels too high?

(**GRETCHEN** *lights a cigarette. Takes a long drag. She raises her arm. She looks down.*)

Mirror, mirror on the wall. Who's the fairest of them all?

(**GRETCHEN** *puts the cigarette out in her armpit. Then she whips her head up and looks at herself. She smiles. It is a much more innocent smile.*)

GRETCHEN. *(cont.)* Why yes Badger, of course I'll marry you.

(*Lights fade on* **GRETCHEN** *in the girls' bathroom, as they rise, across the stage, on the boys' bathroom.* **BADGER,** *17, looking princely in his dark suit, stands before the mirror with his eyes closed.*)

BADGER. Gretchen, will you marry me?

(**BADGER** *opens his eyes. He recoils at the reflection in the mirror. He closes his eyes.*)

(*in a panic*) It's the right thing to do. The *honorable* thing to do. Your father could marry us himself. My mother, if she's well enough to leave the hospital, could sit in the first row of the parish. My God, that would make my Mama proud to be at the front of the church. She thinks Jesus doesn't see so well, on account of his bleedin' eyes. I try to tell her, Mama, that's ridiculous, that isn't the real Jesus hanging up there, it's a statue. But she still thinks the reason she ain't gotten better is because Jesus don't know she's sick, 'cause he can only see the top of her head.

(*Pause.* **BADGER** *opens his eyes cautiously and looks at his reflection. He breathes a sigh of relief.*)

Good. Say it just like that. And if you don't get this done tonight, you'll be whooping your own ass tomorrow morning faster then you can say –

VOICE. Roy Black?

(**BADGER** *whips around.*)

BADGER. Who's there?

(*The sound of a toilet flushing.* **HOYT,** *18, exits from one of the stalls. He's dressed in jeans, a t-shirt and a tie.*)

HOYT. Hello Badger Biers.

BADGER. Hoyt, man, what the fuck?

HOYT. That was quite a speech. So tonight's the night you're going to propose to Gretchen.

BADGER. *(as if it's obvious)* It's Homecoming, asswipe.

HOYT. I just thought – with what happened at Prom last spring, you might want to keep a low profile from now on at school dances.

BADGER. What do you know?

HOYT. He was my best friend. I cannot believe you are going to marry his sister.

BADGER. Do you have a date to this thing? Or do you spend all your Saturday nights in the boys' locker room?

HOYT. Laurel Buchanan.

BADGER. No shit? She's kinda hot.

HOYT. You think so?

BADGER. I did. Until I found out she's dating a loser like you.

HOYT. She's not. We're just here as friends. Laurel only dates Ph.D. candidates.

(Beat. The boys look at each other in the mirror.)

BADGER. I'm sorry man, I didn't mean – you just freaked me out, coming out of the stall like that.

HOYT. Don't do it, man. Don't propose to her. He's coming back. I know he is.

(BADGER punches the wall next to HOYT's head. Hard.)

BADGER. You know *nothing* about me. Do you hear me? NOTHING. And if I ever catch you eavesdropping on a conversation that I am having with myself or anybody else again I will make sure you cannot leave this bathroom without a catheter.

HOYT. Ooh, I'm scared.

(BADGER hits the wall, lightly this time, and exits.)

(HOYT looks down. He's peed himself.)

HOYT. Fuck.

(Lights down.)

(Lights up, at the HOMECOMING DANCE in the gym. **LIBBY** *and* **COSTEN** *are dancing. They are both dressed in southern, high school, formal wear.)*

COSTEN. You look hot, Libby.

LIBBY. Thanks.

(beat)

COSTEN. Do you think I look hot?

LIBBY. What? Oh yeah. Definitely. Really hot.

COSTEN. When someone gives you a compliment, it's nice to pay them one in return.

LIBBY. You're right.

COSTEN. That's called courtesy.

LIBBY. You're right. I'm sorry.

COSTEN. My mother always says the way you tell a person with heritage from a person without, is courtesy. A person with heritage is always courteous. Patient. They know how to wait. They hold doors for women. They sip their cocktails. Because they know, when the sun goes down at the end of that day, they will still be on top. They will still have their heritage, no matter if they've moved forward that day or backwards or nowhere at all. Whereas, someone without heritage has to keep moving forward or they will die. Like sharks.

*(***COSTEN*** *smiles at* **LIBBY***. Then he opens his mouth and bites down violently. Like a shark.* **LIBBY** *has no idea what to say.)*

When you get scared your posture improves.

*(***COSTEN*** *slides his hand down the back of* **LIBBY***'s dress.)*

LIBBY. Stop it!

COSTEN. You know you like it. I really, really want to have sex with you tonight. It's always been a sort of fantasy of mine to do it on the football field. What do you say?

LIBBY. Does heritage screw on a football field?

COSTEN. Why don't you let me worry about my heritage and you worry about your virginity? You haven't had any boyfriends or anything before me, right?

LIBBY. I had one.

COSTEN. You did? Does he go to this school?

LIBBY. Yes. Hoyt. Hoyt Monroe?

COSTEN. I don't know him.

LIBBY. Of course you do. He's in our class. You've known him since kindergarten.

COSTEN. Really? I must have chosen to forget him. Is he ugly or something?

LIBBY. How do you choose to forget somebody?

COSTEN. It's easy if you want to. You just have to condition yourself. For example, every time that person pops into your head, think of maggots. You'll stop thinking about them all together in no time. Your brain won't let you. It really works – I've done it before. Remember Gretchen's faggoty little brother? I don't. I mean, I remember she had one, but I can't remember one thing about him. Whenever I try to...maggots. (**COSTEN** *shudders.*) So this other guy, this...

LIBBY. Hoyt.

COSTEN. Did you fuck him?

(pause)

LIBBY. Fuck him? No.

COSTEN. Good for you. I knew you were a good girl. I love good girls. I'll bet you're wearing white panties, aren't you? Don't answer that. I want it to be a surprise. So where do you want to go to church tomorrow?

LIBBY. Church?

COSTEN. I like to end nights like this at church. It's soothing. It makes you feel clean again. When Gretchen and I used to date we would always haul our asses out of bed and get to her father's early sermon on Sunday morning, no matter how late we'd been up fucking. It was very spiritual.

LIBBY. Gretchen's dad preaches at the Southern Methodist church on Briar Hill, right? My mother loves that church.

COSTEN. Yeah, it's beautiful inside. The richest parish in Durham County.

LIBBY. She wants me to be married there.

COSTEN. Whoa, hold up. I'm talking about Sunday morning service, not walking you down the aisle. Besides, I think we should go to your church.

LIBBY. Why?

COSTEN. I just think it would be a little awkward, me showing up with my new girlfriend to Gretchen's father's sermon.

LIBBY. I'm your girlfriend?

COSTEN. Listen sweetheart, whatever gets you through the night.

(**LIBBY** *stops dancing.*)

COSTEN. I was kidding.

LIBBY. I have to go to the bathroom.

COSTEN. That was a joke.

LIBBY. It wasn't funny.

COSTEN. Libby, if you want to be popular – if you want to be my girlfriend, – you're going to have to lighten up. I've been asking myself why a girl as pretty and nice and smart as you has been a loser all these years? Now I get it. You can't take a joke. Hey, come on. It's Homecoming and you're so beautiful, I feel woozy. Come on.

(**COSTEN** *holds out his arms. They resume dancing.*)

LIBBY. We don't go to church. My mother used to, before she met my father. She used to go to your church actually. But my Dad wouldn't go with her and after he died, she never went back.

COSTEN. That wasn't very Christian of him.

LIBBY. He was Jewish.

(**COSTEN** *and* **LIBBY** *stop dancing again.*)

COSTEN. You're serious?

LIBBY. Yes. Still want to fuck?

COSTEN. More than ever.

> *(He kisses her. She winces. They continue dancing. He starts massaging her scalp as if he's checking for lice.)*

COSTEN. Oh Libby. Libby Sunday. My Jewish princess.

LIBBY. Costen, what are you doing?

COSTEN. You have a very smooth head, Libby.

> *(**BADGER** enters, rubbing his fist.)*

BADGER. Where's Gretchen?

COSTEN. I think she went to the bathroom.

LIBBY. By herself? She's in there by herself? What is she, crazy? We're not supposed to do that anymore. *(beat)* I'll be right back.

COSTEN. Don't be long, sweetheart.

> *(**LIBBY** exits towards the bathroom.)*

I fucked her in the limo ride over.

BADGER. Really?

COSTEN. Almost.

> *(**ROSE** crosses behind **COSTEN** in her moonlight dress. She waves at **BADGER** and disappears into the shadows. **BADGER** is mesmerized.)*

BADGER. I'm gonna go for a walk.

COSTEN. I'm going to stay here and look hot.

> *(**BADGER** exits. Lights down on the GYM.)*
>
> *(Lights rise in the BATHROOM where **GRETCHEN** is still in front of the mirror, as we've left her.)*
>
> *(**LIBBY** enters.)*

LIBBY. Gretchen! There you are. What's that smell?

GRETCHEN. What are you wearing?

LIBBY. Your mom gave it to my mom.

GRETCHEN. My mother gave you my dress?

LIBBY. She said you'd never wear it again.

GRETCHEN. Well look at me – I gave you my guy, I gave you my dress – we really are new best friends, aren't we?

LIBBY. I'd like us to be Gretchen.

GRETCHEN. Why?

LIBBY. I think you're…really nice.

(*Beat.* GRETCHEN *stares at* LIBBY.)

GRETCHEN. So, it seems to me, you and Costen are as cozy as a pig in mud. I did you quite the favor, making that match.

LIBBY. He tried to rape me in the limo ride over.

GRETCHEN. What did you say?

LIBBY. Rape me. Costen tried to rape me.

GRETCHEN. What do you mean?

LIBBY. I mean, he pulled up my dress –

GRETCHEN. That's my dress.

LIBBY. Sorry *your* dress – and pulled down his fly and tried to climb on top of me.

GRETCHEN. Did you fuck him?

LIBBY. No, of course not.

GRETCHEN. He stopped?

LIBBY. I screamed.

GRETCHEN. And he stopped?

LIBBY. Yes.

GRETCHEN. Doesn't sound like he was trying to rape you then.

LIBBY. He had his dick out.

GRETCHEN. You shouldn't toss that word around so carelessly, Libby. That word can destroy a young person's life.

LIBBY. So can being raped.

GRETCHEN. *(considers that)* No, not in the same way. Bodies heal. Babies can be aborted. But reputations? That shit never goes away. Your children's children pay for that. *(beat)* So did you get a look?

LIBBY. At what?

GRETCHEN. His dick.

LIBBY. Sort of.

GRETCHEN. Isn't it beautiful?

LIBBY. I've seen better.

GRETCHEN. Oh please.

LIBBY. I have.

GRETCHEN. You. Libby Sunday. Libby Sunday has seen more than one dick.

LIBBY. I did exist before we became best friends, Gretchen.

GRETCHEN. No, you didn't. *(beat)* Look, don't worry. Costen can't get it up after more than five drinks.

LIBBY. He's not drinking tonight. He wants to be sober to accept the Homecoming crown. When he gets drunk, his eyes cross and his father will tar and feather him if he's looking out all cross-eyed from the picture in tomorrow's paper.

GRETCHEN. Badger is going to be Homecoming king.

LIBBY. Costen doesn't think so.

GRETCHEN. Badger is the captain of the football team. The captain of the football team is always the Homecoming king. It's tradition.

LIBBY. Costen doesn't think Badger is an appropriate role model.

*(Beat. **GRETCHEN** stares at **LIBBY** until icicles form on her lashes.)*

LIBBY. I'm sorry, I –

GRETCHEN. When Costen's the king, I assume you'll be his queen?

LIBBY. *(with a sigh)* Like you said – it's tradition.

GRETCHEN. It's also traditional for the king and queen of the Homecoming dance to get married.

LIBBY. Very funny.

GRETCHEN. I'm not kidding, darling. That's the way it's been every year since Reconstruction. As Homecoming King and Queen it's your responsibility to set a proper Christian example for the other young folks. You get engaged at Homecoming and you're married at Prom. Everyone who's ever been to Prom knows that. Oh, but that's right, you weren't popular last year, so you weren't there.

LIBBY. Can I tell you the truth? I don't even want to be Homecoming Queen.

GRETCHEN. No!

LIBBY. It's true. I'm happy just to be here. With all of you. I don't need a crown. You should have it.

GRETCHEN. Why Libby – that is very generous of you.

LIBBY. I'll go talk to Costen.

GRETCHEN. Would you? Gee, that'd be swell. I'm so glad we're friends. Can I have my dress back first?

LIBBY. This dress?

GRETCHEN. I love that dress. I will wear it again. And even if I don't. I want it back.

LIBBY. You want it back now?

GRETCHEN. Right now. You should tell your mother it's rude to accept hand-outs.

LIBBY. But Gretch, I don't have anything else to wear.

GRETCHEN. Did you really think you could waltz into the ball with my ex-boyfriend in my old dress and claim my crown? Take it off. Or I'll take it off for you.

(Shaking, **LIBBY** *unzips her dress and steps out of it. She hands it to* **GRETCHEN.***)*

LIBBY. I said I'd talk to Costen for you.

*(***GRETCHEN** *sets the dress on fire.)*

GRETCHEN. He wouldn't have listened to you, Libby. He doesn't care what you want. But it's going to be difficult for him to accept Homecoming King when his date is trapped in the bathroom in her training bra and a diaper that says Saturday.

(**GRETCHEN** *hands the burning dress to* **LIBBY** *who puts it out in the sink.*)

LIBBY. It's not a diaper. It's Hanes Her Way Days of the Week underwear.

GRETCHEN. Grow up. Wear a thong.

(**GRETCHEN** *exits.*)

(**LIBBY** *glances at the mirror in fear, then covers her eyes. She huddles on the floor, next to the door, her knees to her chest.*)

(*A knock on the door.*)

LAUREL'S VOICE. Is anyone in there?

LIBBY. Laurel?

LAUREL. Who wants to know?

(**LAUREL** *enters, wearing a beautiful Asian kimono. She's not Asian, just alternative.*)

(*She takes in* **LIBBY** *on the floor.*)

LAUREL. What's the matter? Your dress make you look too fat?

LIBBY. It was Gretchen Black's. She took it back and set it on fire.

(**LAUREL** *smiles.*)

LAUREL. You could cover yourself with my coat.

LIBBY. I could?

(**LAUREL** *takes off her coat and hands it to* **LIBBY.**)

LAUREL. Would you mind? I can see all your ribs and I'm afraid it's going to kill my buzz.

(**LAUREL** *takes out a little bag filled with weed and rolling papers. She sits down on the bench behind* **LIBBY** *and starts to roll a joint.* **LIBBY** *gingerly stands up and wraps the coat around herself. She takes a deep breath and makes herself look into the mirror. She breathes a sigh of relief.* **LAUREL** *notices.*)

It doesn't happen when there's more than one person in the room.

(**LIBBY** *smiles into the MIRROR and nods.*)

LIBBY. *(to the MIRROR)* Who are you here with?

LAUREL. Are you talking to me or yourself?

(**LIBBY** *turns away from the MIRROR.*)

LIBBY. You, of course. Sorry, I just – I haven't seen myself in a while. How are you?

LAUREL. Oh, because, for a moment, I thought maybe the latest "cool kid" thing to do is to talk to all those people who aren't cool, through mirrors. That way, you can pretend like they're your imaginary friends, that you don't actually have to acknowledge in the hallways or hang out with after school, like real people, because they are only figments of your imagination that you can conjure up at whim, through bathroom mirrors, when you're lonely and when you know you're alone.

LIBBY. Laurel – come on.

LAUREL. To hell in your handbasket? No thank you. I may not be in Homecoming court this year, but at least I don't have to blow Costen Lyons at the end of the night.

LIBBY. He tried to…coerce me into having sex with him in the limo ride over.

LAUREL. Of course he did. You're on a date with Costen fucking Lyons. What did you expect?

LIBBY. I thought it might be fun. *(beat)* Are you having fun?

LAUREL. Right now? At Homecoming? Are you kidding? I can't have fun at Homecoming, I would implode. It's the culmination of high school, which itself is the culmination of everything that's ever been wrong with the world since the triumph of Christianity. I am having a delightfully miserable time, of course. It's like being trapped in the middle of a never-ending Philip Larkin poem.

LIBBY. Who?

LAUREL. He's a poet. I'll lend you his stuff as soon as you finally return that copy of *Where the Sidewalk Ends* you borrowed in second grade. Take your time though. It's a big book.

(**LAUREL** *takes a drag.*)

LIBBY. Remember last year's Homecoming, when we broke into the Black family stables and rode the horses over Briar Hill down to the lake?

LAUREL. I remember Hoyt kept screaming that he couldn't feel his balls.

LIBBY. Remember the lake? With the millions of moons floating on the water?

LAUREL. It was pretty beautiful.

LIBBY. It was magic. Roy was magic.

LAUREL. Oh please. He was clever.

LIBBY. Clever people can't break apart the moon.

LAUREL. They can if they hang mirrors from the trees. Do you mean to tell me you never figured that out? I cannot believe you are going to be valedictorian. You are the thickest person I know. How can you possibly get straight As?

LIBBY. I'm detail-oriented. *(casually)* How's Hoyt?

(**LAUREL** *takes another drag.*)

LAUREL. What are you doing?

LIBBY. What? We're just catching up.

LAUREL. We're not friends.

LIBBY. We've been friends since nursery school!

LAUREL. You jumped ship. The moment Roy disappeared.

LIBBY. I needed some space. You and Hoyt were walking around like the sun had gone out. You made me feel like a horrible person if I cracked a smile.

LAUREL. You are a horrible person.

LIBBY. I had to grieve in my own way –

LAUREL. By giving Costen head?

LIBBY. Just because I didn't think we would reach him through a séance –

LAUREL. It worked for James Merrill. He's another poet –

LIBBY. I KNEW THAT.

LAUREL. No you didn't. Look, as much fun as I've had reminiscing with you, I have so much more misery to disseminate tonight, before my work here is through. So, if you'll excuse me…

LIBBY. Have you heard from Roy?

LAUREL. Not since the fruitcake he sent over the holidays.

LIBBY. If there's anything I can do –

LAUREL. Oh Jesus Libby, shut the fuck up.

(LAUREL takes a drag.)

LIBBY. Can I have a hit?

LAUREL. No.

LIBBY. Why not?

LAUREL. Because WE'RE NOT FRIENDS.

LIBBY. Fine. Can you at least tell Hoyt I said hi?

LAUREL. I can do that. Easily. He's my date.

(beat)

LIBBY. What?

LAUREL. Hoyt. I came with Hoyt. He's my date.

LIBBY. Oh. That's funny because Hoyt used to say he would only go to the Homecoming dance if they would be holding public executions there.

LAUREL. I know. He took some convincing. I told him it was either this or the Debutante, but he had to come with me to one of them. He chose this.

LIBBY. You're gonna deb?

LAUREL. Yes, my grandmother sits on the state board, she would disown me if I didn't do it, I need her money for college, resistance is futile, its only one night. Don't look at me like that. What?

LIBBY. That's great.

LAUREL. Yeah, it will be awesome. We can get together beforehand and paint each other's nails and tie each other's twats shut so people think we're virgins.

LIBBY. I wasn't invited.

LAUREL. You're lucky.

LIBBY. It must be fun to be here with Hoyt.

LAUREL. It would be. If he wasn't spending the whole time staring at you.

(*LAUREL takes one last drag of her joint, then extinguishes and puts it back in her pocketbook. She starts to exit. She turns back.*)

LAUREL. Stay here. I'll find you a dress.

(*LAUREL leaves the BATHROOM. LIBBY stares in the mirror.*)

LIBBY. Mirror, mirror on the wall. Who's the fairest of them all?

(*The MIRROR shows LIBBY a reflection that upsets her. She gasps. She turns on her heels and goes into one of the bathroom stalls. The sound of gagging, vomiting and then a toilet being flushed. LIBBY reemerges, pale and shaking.*)

Mirror, mirror on the wall. Who's the fairest of them all?

(*The MIRROR shows LIBBY another reflection. She smiles, weakly.*)

LIBBY. (*cont.*) (*whispering*) Thank you.

(*Lights down in the BATHROOM.*)

(*Lights up in the AUDITORIUM. HOYT is sitting on the stage in his tee-shirt, the tie, and his boxers. He is studying his non-alcoholic punch. LAUREL enters.*)

LAUREL. Hoyt, what are you doing in the auditorium?

HOYT. Squandering my youth.

LAUREL. Is that going to take all night?

HOYT. It's going to take much longer. In the meantime, there must be some way to speed up the fermentation process in this grape juice. Want to go break into the chemistry lab and see what we can accomplish?

LAUREL. What happened to your pants?

HOYT. They got wet. I took them off.

LAUREL. Well put them back on and let's go dance.

(**HOYT** *gives her an "are you crazy" look?*)

LAUREL. You have to dance with me at some point tonight.

HOYT. I said I'd come. I never said I'd dance.

LAUREL. The gym is packed. Nobody will even notice us.

HOYT. Hey, remember Homecoming night last year?

(beat)

LAUREL. *(lying)* Not really.

HOYT. How could you forget? Roy and I hung those mirrors in the trees over Moonlight Lake until the water was bobbing with moons. That was the first night Libby gave me a – that was the best night of my life. *(beat)* Though this is a close second.

LAUREL. I remember you were terribly concerned about the state of your balls on that horse.

HOYT. *(smiling at the memory)* Was I? Yeah, well it turns out they were fine. *(beat)* I cannot *believe* she came with Costen Lyons.

LAUREL. I have a joint in my purse. Want to go hotbox in the car?

HOYT. No thanks. I don't want to do anything that could null this perfectly exquisite pain. (**HOYT** *takes a deep breath.*) Now this is living!

LAUREL. She's a moron.

HOYT. I know.

LAUREL. And two-faced.

HOYT. That's true.

LAUREL. And a shameless social-climber.

HOYT. Utterly remorseless.

LAUREL. So why –

HOYT. *(in agony)* I don't know! Okay? I have no fucking idea.

LAUREL. Hoyt, how often do you think about sex?

HOYT. Ceaselessly.

LAUREL. Me too. I don't know how to stop. Every moment in the day that does not require a hundred and ten percent of my mental capacity – which at this school happens just about never – every other moment there is some part of my brain thinking about sex. Nothing dirty. Not like a porno. Just images. Not even images, but flashes of –

HOYT. Feeling. I know what you mean.

LAUREL. I had this revelation recently. At swim team practice, actually. Watching him cut the water. That this is why Greeks thought young men were beautiful. Because they have bodies like water flowing. Their muscles fit together, work together, follow each other like waves. And I thought, Oh Sophocles. I get you man. I really get you.

HOYT. Watching who cut the water?

LAUREL. Nobody.

HOYT. No wonder you always swim in the guys' lane. I thought you wanted to challenge yourself.

LAUREL. Fuck off, I said.

HOYT. Who is it? Come on, you have to tell me.

LAUREL. It's you Hoyt.

HOYT. Very funny. Tell me who it really is. Maybe I can help. Badger Biers thinks you're really hot. But I told him you only date Ph.D. candidates.

(*A beat.* **LAUREL** *stares at* **HOYT**.)

LAUREL. Thanks for that.

HOYT. Does it ever strike you as a bad joke? Life?

LAUREL. I'm not sure we're qualified to judge whether or not this is all suppose to be ironic yet. We're only seventeen.

HOYT. I'm eighteen.

LAUREL. Oh, well, in that case, how does it look from there?

HOYT. Bleak. What's the point? We all hate each other. We derive pleasure from hurting each other. Who green-lighted this project? Who woke up and said "Mankind, now that's a good idea." I'd just like to know.

LAUREL. Come on, let's go ask pot. Pot will know.

(LAUREL and HOYT start to exit the AUDITORIUM. LAUREL stops short.)

I had a reason for coming here. What was it? Oh, that's right. The costume closet.

HOYT. You need a costume?

LAUREL. I need a dress.

HOYT. I like the one you have on.

LAUREL. You do? Really?

HOYT. Yeah. For a culturally appropriated sartorial statement, it's not as offensive as it could be.

LAUREL. Thank you, Hoyt. That was practically a compliment. But it's not for me. It's for your ex-girlfriend. She's naked in the women's bathroom and she's freezing.

HOYT. Why?

LAUREL. Probably because she's anorexic.

HOYT. I meant, why is she naked?

LAUREL. I don't know, Hoyt. Why is she valedictorian? Why did she dump you for Costen Lyons? Why doesn't she eat? I'll be honest with you – I don't get her. But I promised I'd bring her something to wear. I'll be right back.

(LAUREL exits into the costume closet.)

(Behind HOYT, ROSE opens the door to the auditorium and peeks in.)

HOYT. I wish Roy were here. He'd know how to ferment the grape juice.

(ROSE jumps a little and quickly exits.)

(LAUREL reemerges with a Cinderella dress.)

LAUREL. Recognize this?

HOYT. It's the Cinderella costume.

LAUREL. You think Libby could pull it off?

HOYT. I'm the wrong person to ask. Libby could pull a diaper off as far as I'm concerned.

LAUREL. You know what your problem is, Hoyt? You're just like all the rest of them. You're a sheep in wolf's clothing. I am the only truly, authentically cool person I know. I am so alone.

HOYT. Why don't you write a poem about it?

(LAUREL stares at HOYT, furious. Then she turns on her heels and then starts to exit.)

HOYT. Laurel, wait!

LAUREL. What?

HOYT. Can I give bring Libby the dress?

LAUREL. No!

(At the door, LAUREL bumps right into BADGER BIERS.)

BADGER. Hey. Did y'all see a girl come through here in a dress the color of moonlight?

(LAUREL and HOYT look at each other, amazed.)

LAUREL. Ah, no. Sorry.

BADGER. Damn. I could have sworn she came this way. What is this place anyway?

LAUREL. The auditorium.

BADGER. Oh *this* is the auditorium. This is where you all do those…those…

HOYT. Plays?

BADGER. Right. Right. Sort of creepy in here, isn't it?

LAUREL. I was just heading back to the gym. Care to walk me?

BADGER. My pleasure.

(BADGER offers LAUREL his arm.)

BADGER. So you didn't see no new girl?

LAUREL. 'Fraid not, honeychild.

(*As* BADGER *and* LAUREL *exit,* LAUREL *raises her free hand to flip* HOYT *off.*)

(HOYT *sighs, takes out a book and lies down on stage. Lights down in the auditorium.*)

(*Lights up on the* HOMECOMING *dance.* BADGER *and* LAUREL *enter.* GRETCHEN *is waiting in the middle of the floor. She waves.* BADGER *goes to* GRETCHEN. LAUREL *continues towards the bathroom.*)

BADGER. There you are.

GRETCHEN. Where've you been?

BADGER. Me? You're the one who's been in the bathroom all night.

GRETCHEN. I had to check my face…this is a big night for us, Badger.

(BADGER *looks around the room.*)

GRETCHEN. Who are you looking for?

BADGER. What? Nobody. No one. Why?

GRETCHEN. Are you going to dance with me?

(BADGER *takes* GRETCHEN *in his arms. He smiles at her. They begin dancing.*)

BADGER. Of course, I don't know what I was – this is great. Isn't this great? This is so great. We're at Homecoming.

GRETCHEN. Ow! Watch it, these are open-toed shoes.

BADGER. You look so great. Your skin feels so great. Your hair smells so –

(BADGER *smells* GRETCHEN*'s hair.*)

(*coldly*) Have you been smoking?

GRETCHEN. No! You know I don't smoke, baby.

BADGER. Your hair smells like smoke.

GRETCHEN. That's because girls like the one you came in with are puffing away in the bathroom.

BADGER. Who, Laurel?

GRETCHEN. Is that her name?

BADGER. She's in Cotillion Class with us.

GRETCHEN. Is she? I never noticed.

BADGER. She's one of Costen's second cousins. Her family basically founded this county. And she doesn't smoke cigarettes. Though she has experimented with marijuana.

GRETCHEN. How do you know that?

BADGER. I talk to her when we're partnered in Cotillion.

GRETCHEN. You never talk to me in Cotillion.

BADGER. You make me nervous.

GRETCHEN. I make you nervous? You're the one who can't dance.

> *(beat)*

BADGER. Cigarettes killed my mother.

GRETCHEN. They haven't killed her yet, baby. I thought she looked so sweet in that African headdress thing she had on when she took our picture. I'd've never known she had cancer, if I didn't know already. I'd've thought she was an African princess.

BADGER. Africans are black.

GRETCHEN. Not their princesses.

BADGER. Their princesses too. Everyone is black.

GRETCHEN. Then how do they tell the princesses apart from the regular folk?

BADGER. They recognize them.

GRETCHEN. You sure they aren't white people who just look dark because of all the sun they get?

> *(**BADGER** stops dancing.)*

Oh Badger, I'm kidding. Give me a little credit. I'm not a total moron. I was just trying to say something nice about your mother.

BADGER. Don't bother. She's dying. She looks like shit.

GRETCHEN. That's not true.

BADGER. YES IT IS.

> *(**GRETCHEN** and **BADGER** stop dancing.)*

GRETCHEN. Baby? Don't get upset. It's okay –

BADGER. Have they announced the king and queen?

GRETCHEN. Not yet.

BADGER. When is that going to happen?

GRETCHEN. Soon.

BADGER. Do we have to stay until that happens?

GRETCHEN. Considering it's going to be us, I think we should stay, don't you?

BADGER. Why don't we just get it over with now?

GRETCHEN. Get what over with?

(BADGER *takes* GRETCHEN's *hand and drops down to one knee.*)

BADGER. Gretchen Black, will you –

(*Behind* GRETCHEN, ROSE *appears. She waves at* BADGER *and exits out the gym door.*)

– Will you give me a second?

(BADGER *exits after* ROSE *just as* COSTEN *enters.*)

COSTEN. Gretchen, where's my date?

GRETCHEN. How the hell should I know?

COSTEN. Because she got all freaked out when you went to the bathroom by yourself and she went to find you. Apparently, she's one of those "really nice people." And now you're here and she's nowhere to be seen. So what did you do to her?

GRETCHEN. Nothing. I never saw her.

COSTEN. People don't just vanish.

(GRETCHEN *looks off to where* BADGER *exited.*)

GRETCHEN. Around here they do.

(COSTEN *follows* GRETCHEN's *gaze.*)

COSTEN. I think you ought to let him go, Gretch. After what happened at Prom last year, this can't be easy for him.

GRETCHEN. *(slowly)* I have no idea what you're talking about, I'm sure.

COSTEN. I own this town. It keeps no secrets from me. The tobacco leaves tell me everything.

GRETCHEN. If you're Homecoming King, you'll have to propose to Libby.

COSTEN. You could have told me she was Jewish.

GRETCHEN. I thought you knew. Everyone knows.

COSTEN. That's why nobody's touched her so far.

GRETCHEN. Right.

COSTEN. She's such a pretty girl.

GRETCHEN. And her cunt works fine, Costen. Don't sweat it.

COSTEN. If I didn't know better, I'd say you were jealous.

GRETCHEN. You know better.

COSTEN. Remember when we used to be in love?

GRETCHEN. We were never in love. We were neighbors who fucked.

COSTEN. Why do you insist on fighting your destiny, my love? Be my queen and together we will rule these sweet, low lands.

(LIBBY *reemerges from the BATHROOM in a Cinderella dress.*)

COSTEN. *(to* LIBBY*)* Princess, you changed!

(BADGER *suddenly reappears in the doorway of the GYM. He looks strangely pale. Perhaps the lighting shifts for a moment.*)

BADGER. Y'all ain't gonna believe this. But outside there's blue snow falling. Take a look.

COSTEN. Blue snow? Are you shitting me? My Granddaddy says that hasn't happened since all the darkies rose into the air and flew away in the Christmas of 1848.

(COSTEN *takes* LIBBY *and* GRETCHEN*'s hands and leads them outside.*)

GRETCHEN. Badger?

BADGER. I'll be right there, baby. I just need to use the bathroom.

GRETCHEN. Want me to come?

BADGER. I'll be okay. Go ahead.

> (*GRETCHEN,* **COSTEN** *and* **LIBBY** *exit.*)

> (**BADGER** *is alone for a moment in the center of the empty GYM. A figure appears in the doorway behind him, silhouetted in blue. It's* **ROSE.** *They move toward each other as if in a trance. The moment they meet, they begin to waltz, sweeping around the space.*)

BADGER. Rose? Rose what?

ROSE. Rose White.

BADGER. That's the most beautiful name I've ever heard.

ROSE. What's yours again?

BADGER. Badger. Badger Biers. It's a family name.

ROSE. It suits you.

BADGER. I feel funny. With you in my arms. Like I'm drunk or something. Where are you from?

ROSE. The south.

BADGER. The real south?

ROSE. Yes sir.

BADGER. I've heard the wells are filled with sweet tea – is it true?

ROSE. I shower in sweet tea every morning and take an evening bath of oatmeal. That's what keeps my skin so smooth.

BADGER. I've heard there's nothing to do but eat and sleep and make love.

ROSE. And read and dance.

BADGER. Oh. I didn't know about all that. I'm mighty poor at both. I wouldn't last a moment –

ROSE. I think you're a right fine dancer, Badger Biers.

BADGER. I know – it's strange. I'm usually awful. But somehow, leading you is as easy as dreaming.

ROSE. Silly darling, I'm leading you.

BADGER. No you're not. Wait, yes you are! I didn't even notice. How are you doing that?

ROSE. I told you. I'm from the REAL south.

BADGER. Why would you leave such a place?

ROSE. You mustn't stay anywhere too long, Badger Biers. You're liable to grow roots like a tree and be stuck.

BADGER. Nobody ever leaves this county.

ROSE. Nobody?

BADGER. Well, somebody did once. But he didn't belong here anyhow.

ROSE. Why not?

BADGER. He was sinful.

(LIBBY *reenters, missing one shoe. She hobbles over to them.*)

LIBBY. Have y'all seen Hoyt?

BADGER. Libby, this is Rose. She's new.

LIBBY. Nice to meet you. Where you from?

ROSE. The south.

BADGER. The Deep South.

LIBBY. Right. Badger, have you seen Hoyt?

BADGER. What happened to your other shoe?

LIBBY. I don't know. It fell off in the blue snow. It was white, so I thought it would show up somewhere in the drifts, but I can't find it and I'm getting frostbite and I don't feel well and I just want to go home. I was hoping Hoyt could drive me.

ROSE. I think he's in the auditorium.

(LIBBY *and* BADGER *stare at her, strangely.*)

LIBBY. Do you know Hoyt?

ROSE. No, but there's a boy sitting alone in the auditorium.

LIBBY. What did he look like?

ROSE. Cute. In a tee-shirt and a tie, reading Albert Camus in the original French.

LIBBY. That's Hoyt. Thanks.

(LIBBY *starts to exit.*)

ROSE. And the snow is actually white. It's the moon that's blue.

*(**LIBBY** considers this.)*

LIBBY. I don't think so.

*(**GRETCHEN** appears silhouetted in the doorway. She stares at **BADGER** and **ROSE** hatefully.)*

GRETCHEN. Libby. Bathroom. Now.

LIBBY. Fuck.

*(**LIBBY** turns around and hobbles into the BATHROOM after **GRETCHEN**.)*

BADGER. I can't help feeling like we've met before.

ROSE. We have. In a past life.

*(**COSTEN** enters the GYM.)*

COSTEN. Dude, man, that was friggin' beautiful. Where's Gretchen?

BADGER. They're in the bathroom.

ROSE. *(lightly)* Why must girls always go to the bathroom in groups?

(pause)

COSTEN. Who the fuck are you?

BADGER. Costen, this is Rose. She's new. *(to **ROSE**)* There's something wrong with the mirrors around here.

COSTEN. Have we fucked?

BADGER. Whoa! Dude!

COSTEN. Did I just say that aloud? What is the matter with me? That was so *uncourteous*. It's the little Jewish girl's fault. She put some kind of spell on me. Fucking horn-less witch. I hope she screamed like hell when they sawed those things off. Would you excuse me? I have to go purify.

BADGER. What are you going to do?

COSTEN. Cleanse myself. Burn something.

BADGER. Some*thing*, right Costen? Not some*one*?

COSTEN. Right, right. Don't worry. I got it. *(to **ROSE**)* Pleasure to meet you.

ROSE. You as well.

(COSTEN exits.)

BADGER. I hope he didn't upset you.

ROSE. Not at all.

BADGER. Let's get out of here. Just you and me. You're the most beautiful girl in the world.

ROSE. What about your girlfriend?

BADGER. Who Gretchen? Oh, she's not my girlfriend.

ROSE. Don't lie to me Badger, I was just starting to like you.

BADGER. Okay, fine, she is. But we're about to break up.

ROSE. Sure you are.

BADGER. We are. I swear it. I'm a born-again virgin and she's a sex fiend. Our relationship has no growth potential.

ROSE. She doesn't look like a sex fiend.

BADGER. She's had a tough couple of years.

ROSE. So she's become addicted to sex?

BADGER. There's this guy, Plato? I think he's dead, but he had this theory. He said a woman's womb was like an animal living inside her that had to be beaten down by a penis regularly otherwise it would climb up through her spine and eat her brain. I know he sort of sounds like an asshole, but he was right about Gretchen.

ROSE. What's the matter with her?

BADGER. Her real Dad accidentally shot himself hunting and her mom remarried this minister who likes to come into her room at night and stare at her while she's sleeping. And then one day, she saw her brother doing something stupid and she didn't know what to do, so she told her mother who told her stepfather who made her brother disappear. Now I come over every so often and she takes me down to the lake and we do it on the old dock until she bleeds.

ROSE. She bleeds?

BADGER. I don't think she enjoys it very much and I know I sure as hell don't, but it does seem to calm her down and she's an old friend.

ROSE. What was her brother doing?

BADGER. *(harshly)* How should I know?

    (pause)

ROSE. Did you know him?

BADGER. A bit.

ROSE. Did you love him?

    (BADGER stops dancing.)

BADGER. What?

ROSE. Did you love her?

BADGER. Who?

ROSE. Gretchen. Do you love her?

BADGER. Oh, I thought you said – never mind. No, I don't love – I wish I did. Somebody should. Now that her brother is gone, she hasn't got anyone. But not me. It can't be me. We know each other way too well.

ROSE. Then dump her.

    (ROSE smiles at BADGER. He smiles back tentatively. LIGHTS fade on the gym.)

    (LIGHT rise in the BATHROOM.)

    (GRETCHEN and LIBBY are sitting on the benches, staring at each other.)

LIBBY. Gretch? Gretch? Are we just going to sit here for the rest of the night?

GRETCHEN. Do you have a better idea?

LIBBY. It's damp in here. Won't our hair frizz?

GRETCHEN. Do you think she was wearing make-up?

LIBBY. Who?

GRETCHEN. I mean, could anyone's lips really be that red when their skin is so pale?

LIBBY. She was probably wearing make-up.

GRETCHEN. Right, but then, wouldn't it bleed?

LIBBY. What?

GRETCHEN. The lipstick. The red lipstick. Wouldn't it bleed into the white foundation?

LIBBY. Not if she put liner on first.

GRETCHEN. Some girls wear entirely too much makeup. There's a trick with makeup. The trick is, you always want to look like you just had sex. My mother taught me that when I was young. She said, "Gretchen study your After Sex Face and then try to replicate it." It's a dance really, between the red and the white. The foundation and the flush. The virgin and the whore.

LIBBY. I was thinking, maybe after this is over, we could all go play mini putt-putt.

GRETCHEN. Mini putt-putt?

LIBBY. They keep the one over on Stagecoach Road open until midnight on Saturdays.

GRETCHEN. Libby, after Homecoming we're going back to Costen's house. We're going to get trashed and fuck our boyfriends.

LIBBY. We are?

GRETCHEN. Of course. It's Homecoming! And in the morning, we all get up and go to my father's church.

LIBBY. In that case, I think I might just go home.

GRETCHEN. Why?

LIBBY. I have a lot of homework to do this weekend.

GRETCHEN. You're a virgin aren't you?

LIBBY. No.

GRETCHEN. Of course you are. Don't worry. Costen loves virgins. He's sort of an expert on them. I'll give you a Valium for the pain.

LIBBY. I'm going home.

GRETCHEN. Don't be such a scaredy cat, Libby. You'll be drunk and drugged – you won't feel a thing.

LIBBY. It's not that. I just don't think I'm cut out for being popular. I'm sorry. You've been very nice to me. Thanks for letting me date your ex-boyfriend and do your homework for you and lend you tampons and everything. I've had a very nice time. I have to go now though.

GRETCHEN. Are you crazy? You're going to ditch Costen in the middle of Homecoming? He will make your life hell.

LIBBY. I'm not scared.

GRETCHEN. You should be. You have no idea what you're up against. His family owns this town.

LIBBY. *(on the verge of tears)* I'm so tired. I just want to go home.

GRETCHEN. Are you crying? You can't cry. Your mascara will run and we'll be here all night. Now think happy thoughts.

LIBBY. I got a sixteen-hundred on my SATs.

GRETCHEN. Right, I meant something that would make you seem like less of a loser. Here, just do what I do. It's a little old trick I made up. Works every time. Look in the mirror. Now close your eyes and repeat after me.

*(Both girls close their eyes. **ROSE** enters the bathroom quietly and stands behind them, watching.)*

LIBBY. Is this a good idea?

GRETCHEN. Mirror, mirror.

LIBBY. Mirror, mirror.

GRETCHEN. On the wall.

LIBBY. On the wall.

GRETCHEN. Who's the fairest –

LIBBY. I know this trick.

GRETCHEN & LIBBY. Of them all?

*(Both women open their eyes at the same time and see **ROSE** in the mirror.)*

ROSE. Gretchen, Badger wants to talk to you.

(blackout)

End of Act One

ACT 2

(The MONDAY after HOMECOMING. The LOCKER ROOM.)

(COSTEN is in front of the mirror, in his football pads, wearing a crown. He is trying to fit his football helmet on over the crown.)

(It's not working.)

(COSTEN puts the football helmet down and takes off his crown.)

(The image in the mirror changes.)

(COSTEN swallows hard and puts the crown back on.)

(BADGER saunters in, wearing school clothes.)

(COSTEN looks at his watch, incredulously. BADGER looks at COSTEN's crown in the same way.)

COSTEN. Hi, I'm Costen. I'm on the football team. Who are you?

BADGER. I'm late.

COSTEN. You're dead. Coach is gonna fry your nuts.

BADGER. Nah, he won't. Coach and I understand each other. Are you going to wear that to practice?

COSTEN. *(scornfully)* Of course not. How would I fit it under my helmet?

BADGER. Good point. I guess that means you got Homecoming King. Congratulations.

COSTEN. Oh, you think that's funny, huh?

BADGER. No. I think it's appropriate. Libby must have been thrilled. We've never had a Jewish Homecoming Queen.

COSTEN. And we never will. How come everyone knew she was Jewish but me?

39

BADGER. Libby wasn't the queen?

COSTEN. Dude, where have you been all weekend? Libby had to take Gretch home after you disappeared with that new girl. Which, I got to say, dude, was NOT cool. Leaving your date at Homecoming for another girl? Not at all courteous. Especially for some new girl with no ass or tits to speak of. That girl gave me the creeps, Badge. I'll bet she's Jewish too. It's an invasion. I should tell my father. He'll want to start organizing.

BADGER. Costen, it's not an invasion. Do not tell your father. So if Gretchen and Libby both left, who was the Homecoming Queen?

COSTEN. I don't want to talk about it.

BADGER. Why not? Who was it?

COSTEN. We should get down to the field.

BADGER. Tell me first.

COSTEN. Laurel Buchanan.

BADGER. Your second cousin?

COSTEN. Oh you think that's funny, huh? I freaked, okay? They called my name – actually, first they called your name, but someone said you'd left with the new girl, so then they called my name. I went up there and they asked me to pick a queen, so I called Gretchen – but someone said she'd left with Libby and I freaked. All I could think was "heritage, heritage, heritage" and so I called the only person who's pedigree I was certain of. My second cousin.

BADGER. I think it's great. I love Laurel.

COSTEN. How do you know her?

BADGER. She goes to school here.

COSTEN. So?

BADGER. I sit next to her in chemistry class.

COSTEN. So?

BADGER. Sometime I ask her questions. About our home-work and stuff.

COSTEN. Does she answer?

BADGER. Yes.

COSTEN. Really? She hasn't spoken to me since Junior High. I thought maybe she'd gone deaf.

BADGER. Did she accept the crown?

COSTEN. Yes. Everything was going along fine. We danced. She was wearing something ridiculous but she was actually a decent dancer – it's the pedigree –

BADGER. It's the Cotillion classes.

COSTEN. Is she in those too? You're kidding? We should carpool – her family lives down the block. Anyway, the photographer for the town paper came to take our picture and that little bitch waited until the last possible moment, then stuck out her tongue. (*beat*) It has a bar through it.

BADGER. No!

COSTEN. Yes. My second cousin has married the devil. So, of course they didn't print that picture in the paper on Sunday. Which is why I have to wear this crown everywhere I go. So everyone knows – the king is me.

BADGER. That's tough man, I'm sorry.

COSTEN. Yeah, it was tough, man. I could have really used your support this weekend. Where were you yesterday? Why weren't you at church?

BADGER. I took Rose to Moonlight Lake.

COSTEN. Did you nail her?

BADGER. I don't want to nail her. She won't even let me kiss her. But I don't care. I want to be around her all the time. Sometimes, when I'm with her, I start to laugh. For absolutely no good reason – just because I'm so happy. I look into her face, her dark eyes and she's looking at me so patiently, so serenely, waiting for me to stop so she can continue being lovely – but I can't stop. I laugh until I can't breath. What do you think that means?

COSTEN. She's cursed you.

BADGER. I don't care. I hope she has. I hope I'm under her spell or else, in a dream and I NEVER WAKE UP. I'm in love, dude. Everything around me is so beautiful. You! You are so beautiful.

(**BADGER** *grabs* **COSTEN** *and kisses him on the cheek.*)

COSTEN. *(irate)* What the fuck is wrong with you, faggot?

BADGER. Sorry man – I don't know what came over me. I'll meet you down at the field.

COSTEN. You do that.

(**COSTEN** *grabs his football helmet and exits.*)

(**BADGER**, *takes his football helmet out of his locker. He looks at himself in the mirror. He sees something wrong. He shakes his head.*)

BADGER. That isn't me, man.

(**BADGER** *puts his helmet back in his locker and leaves the locker room.*)

(*Lights down. Lights up in the girls' BATHROOM.*)

(*Enter* **LIBBY** *and* **GRETCHEN**, *now in school clothes. They take out their make-up cases and begin to reapply their make-up.*)

GRETCHEN. I'm telling you, there is something very wrong with her. She isn't normal.

LIBBY. I think she seems nice.

GRETCHEN. She seems like a freak. Look Libby, I've never told this to you, but I have special powers. I can look at any girl and tell you where she is in her menstrual cycle, to the day.

LIBBY. Really?

GRETCHEN. Really. Here I'll do you. *(Pause.* **GRETCHEN** *squints at* **LIBBY**, *hard.)* You haven't had a period for six months because you're anorexic.

LIBBY. Shit.

GRETCHEN. Yeah, I know, it's just something I've always been able to do. I'm a very mystical person. Stick with me and there's all sorts of things I can teach you. I know how to make a boy so hard his balls turn blue.

LIBBY. That's not so hard. Anyone can do –

GRETCHEN. And fall off.

LIBBY. You're kidding.

GRETCHEN. I wish I was. I have one of Costen's balls pickled in a jar beside my bed. Why do you think he blindfolded you?

LIBBY. I'm gonna throw up.

GRETCHEN. Throw up what? What have you eaten today? *(pause)* That's alright. You can think about it and get back to me. I have both of Mr. Cornelius's balls on my desk.

LIBBY. Our science teacher?

GRETCHEN. They're in formaldehyde. They're my graduation insurance. He really wants them back. They're trying to have a kid and all...

LIBBY. Gretchen, that's just...wicked.

GRETCHEN. What else could I do, Libby? I have a learning disability. You smart kids can be so self-righteous. Plastic surgery can make you beautiful, but can I get a brain transplant? No. I was born with a sociological disadvantage that can't be corrected. So pardon me for learning to use what I've got.

LIBBY. I'm sorry.

GRETCHEN. You should be. So, here's the thing. With what's-her-puss, I get nothing.

LIBBY. I'm sorry?

GRETCHEN. And I'm supposed to be the one with the learning disability. The new girl hasn't had her period. Ever.

LIBBY. Are you sure?

GRETCHEN. Yes, of course I'm sure. I told you she was a freak.

LIBBY. Maybe she's just hasn't developed yet.

GRETCHEN. We're seventeen.

LIBBY. It takes some people just a little longer.

GRETCHEN. Why are you defending her?

LIBBY. She doesn't know anybody here and she seems really nice and I just don't understand why we have to hate her. It's not her fault Badger dumped you.

GRETCHEN. Libby, this may sound harsh but I'm only telling you because I actually like you and I want to save you a lot of unnecessary heartache. You will never be cool.

LIBBY. What?

GRETCHEN. I'm sorry. You just don't have what it takes. Now, if you don't mind, go do what you can for that sad little face of yours, somewhere else. You're annoying me.

LIBBY. Why?

GRETCHEN. I don't know. It's something about the way you tied your ponytail this morning. It's a little crooked and it's driving me nuts. Leave.

(A pounding on the door.)

COSTEN. *(offstage)* Gretch, is that you? It's an emergency.

GRETCHEN. Costen?

*(**COSTEN** bursts into the BATHROOM.)*

COSTEN. I told you it was contagious.

GRETCHEN. What are you talking about?

COSTEN. Your brother. His infection. Everyone called it a condition but my Dad said it was a disease and he was right and now Badger has it.

GRETCHEN. That's a vicious lie.

COSTEN. It is fucking not. He just…he just…I can't say it…I can't even think it…he kissed me!

GRETCHEN. Badger kissed you?

COSTEN. He belongs in *public school.* Come on Libby, we have ten minutes to fuck before warm-ups start.

LIBBY. Costen, we're at school. Couldn't we wait until tonight at least?

COSTEN. I have to make sure I'm not infected. Otherwise, how will I concentrate at practice this afternoon? With Badger benched, now's my chance to play quarterback.

GRETCHEN. Coach won't bench Badger. He's the captain.

COSTEN. Gretchen, if Badger had Ebola do you think Coach would start him?

GRETCHEN. That's ridiculous.

COSTEN. My point exactly. Oh come on Libby, we have eight minutes.

(**COSTEN** *drags* **LIBBY** *off.*)

(**GRETCHEN** *looks in the mirror.*)

(*She doesn't like what she sees.*)

GRETCHEN. *(to the mirror)* Stay away from me.

(*She lights another cigarette, takes a few puffs and raises her arm, as in the first scene, when suddenly, the door swings open and* **ROSE** *enters.*)

ROSE. Hi Gretchen. What are you doing?

GRETCHEN. They don't knock where you're from?

ROSE. Not for public bathrooms with more than one stall.

GRETCHEN. Right. This is a private school? Okay?

ROSE. Okay, what?

GRETCHEN. Okay, leave.

(*pause*)

ROSE. Did you have a nice time at Homecoming?

GRETCHEN. Did you not hear what I just said?

ROSE. I had such a nice time at Homecoming. Badger Biers is so cute.

GRETCHEN. Badger Biers is my boyfriend.

ROSE. Are you sure? You might want to check with him.

GRETCHEN. He has been my boyfriend for over a year now. We are the most popular couple in school. We're going to get married.

ROSE. He left Homecoming with me.

GRETCHEN. Badger doesn't like school dances. He thinks they're plebian and I'm inclined to agree with him. It doesn't make sense. Why have a party if you're going to invite everyone? This isn't the first time he's left a school dance early. The same thing happened

GRETCHEN. *(cont.)* last spring at Prom. But it doesn't matter because he ALWAYS comes back to me on Monday. He has no choice. We were meant to be together. We know *everything* about each other. *(beat)* I'm not this nice to everyone. I'm trying to help you.

ROSE. Why?

GRETCHEN. I have no idea. Something about you makes me –

ROSE. Sad?

GRETCHEN. Sick.

ROSE. Jealousy does that to certain girls. I'm not *trying* to hurt you, Gretchen. Sometimes, I just hate being the most beautiful girl in school.

GRETCHEN. I am the most beautiful girl in school.

ROSE. Oh, I'm sorry, I was confused. I didn't realize who you were. Let me try again. You're so beautiful, I wish I could be you.

GRETCHEN. That's better.

ROSE. And your boyfriend is so cute, I'm going to fuck him. Oh wait, I messed up. Can I start again?

GRETCHEN. Do you have a death wish?

ROSE. I see right through you, Gretchen. You cry in your sleep just like the rest of us.

GRETCHEN. I will kill you.

ROSE. You'd have no idea how. I am not like other girls.

(**GRETCHEN** *grabs her purse, finds her cell phone and opens it.*)

GRETCHEN. Hello? Oh hey Badger baby. *(to* **ROSE***)* I have to take this.

ROSE. Was it ringing?

GRETCHEN. It's on vibrate, bitch.

(**GRETCHEN** *leaves the bathroom.* **ROSE** *looks at herself in the mirror and reapplies her powder. She smiles at her reflection.*)

ROSE. You look pretty.

(HONEY enters. She's a nerd. She wears thick, plastic glasses and a neon green windbreaker. She doesn't look at ROSE or the MIRROR. She bows her head and washes her hands meticulously in the sink.)

HONEY. One two three. One two three. One two three.

ROSE. Hi, my name's Rose, I'm new here.

HONEY. I know. I noticed you right away. You're hard to miss.

ROSE. Oh?

HONEY. You're just so unique looking.

ROSE. Oh, stop please, you're making me blush.

HONEY. Really? *(She peers closely at Rose's white cheeks).* I can't tell.

ROSE. I was just about to go get a milkshake from the snack shack. Care to join me? I'm sorry, I don't think I caught your name?

HONEY. It's Honey. And I appreciate it, but only if you're sure. I mean, you're new and all. I understand if you want to be careful for a while.

ROSE. I beg your pardon?

HONEY. If you don't want to get off on the wrong foot. Be seen with the wrong people. I should tell you – for the sake of full disclosure – I'm one of the seven dweebs.

ROSE. The seven dweebs. Goodness, who are they?

HONEY. Me, Donnie, Ronnie, Hoyt and Laurel.

ROSE. But that's only five.

HONEY. Right. We were seven. But then Roy disappeared and Libby got popular – I can't, for the life of me, figure out how.

ROSE. Some people just get lucky.

HONEY. You know, that's funny. That's just what my friend Roy use to say.

ROSE. The one who disappeared? Did you know him well?

HONEY. You could say that. I only stared at him every moment I could, every day for ten years. I was sort of in love with him. All the dweeby girls were.

ROSE. Was he very handsome?

HONEY. No. It was something else. He went around smiling at people – indiscriminately and for no good reason. Like we were all children again. It freaked a lot of people out. But it made me shiver all over. It was just so *dangerous*. Once, I was watching him in chemistry class – Roy and I were in that class as sophomores even though it's junior class, because we're gifted and talented – and his sister, Gretchen, was asking the teacher some stupid question about how long things keep in formaldehyde – which had *nothing* to do with the topic at hand – anyway, Roy looked over at Badger Biers and smiled at him. And Badger Biers *sort of smiled back*. It was the most incredible thing I've ever seen. I went home and wrote twelve pages about it in my journal. If Roy hadn't gotten sick I would have asked him to Homecoming.

ROSE. He got sick?

HONEY. Oh yes. Terribly, terribly sick.

ROSE. What did he get?

(**HONEY** *writes something down in her notebook.*)

ROSE. *(reading)* Gay?

(**HONEY** *nods solemnly.*)

ROSE. He got gay?

HONEY. Nobody knows how.

ROSE. Why'd you write it down?

HONEY. Oh, it's silly. My grandmother always says bad things are only true if you say them aloud. She's a little superstitious, but in case she's right, I don't want to hurt Roy.

ROSE. What happened to Roy?

HONEY. My grandmother says, one night, when nobody was looking, the angel Gabriel came and got him and turned him into chewing tar, for being wicked, and his own father chewed him the next morning and spit him out. Ain't that just awful?

ROSE. Do you think that's true?

HONEY. All I know is, the mirrors went demented after last prom and they say it's because one of them caught the sickness from Roy and infected all the others.

ROSE. Let me get this straight – the mirrors are homosexual?

(HONEY jumps.)

HONEY. Where did you say you were from again?

ROSE. Honey, just think about it –

HONEY. I'm sorry Rose, you seem really nice and all but you've got a mouth as dirty as a sailor and it makes me kind of uncomfortable – being a dweeb and all – so I'm gonna go now.

(LIBBY enters and bumps into HONEY as she's leaving.)

LIBBY. Hey Honey.

HONEY. Hi Libby.

LIBBY. How are you?

HONEY. Why are you talking to me?

LIBBY. We just bumped into –

HONEY. What do you want?

LIBBY. Nothing. I miss you. How are –

HONEY. Where's Gretchen Black?

LIBBY. Well, I left her in here.

HONEY. I didn't say anything bad about her.

LIBBY. Were y'all just talking about her or –

HONEY. We were just talking. You should mind your own business.

LIBBY. Honey, can I ask you a favor?

HONEY. I don't know, can you?

LIBBY. Would you let Gretchen copy your chemistry homework?

HONEY. No! That's against all sorts of rules. It explicitly says so in the student constitution – which reminds me – now that you're too cool for student council meetings

HONEY. *(cont.)* you really ought to resign and let someone else be the delegate because your homeroom is *seriously* unrepresented.

LIBBY. That's how Gretchen and I became friends in the first place.

HONEY. Gretchen's not on student council.

LIBBY. I mean, through tutoring. I let her borrow my algebra, then she lent me her mascara and I've been popular ever since.

HONEY. That sounds too easy.

LIBBY. I swear it. There's really nothing to it. Sometimes you need to break a few rules to get a date for Prom.

HONEY. You think I could get a date for the prom?

LIBBY. It's seven months away. I'd say, if you start now, you could have your pick.

HONEY. My pick?!

LIBBY. But listen, you have to start right now. Today. Go down to the Snack Shack and tell Gretchen that I sent you with the intel. She'll understand.

HONEY. Oh wow. I don't know what to say. Thanks Libby. I'll take the pins out of your voodoo doll as soon as I get home.

LIBBY. Honey? You better leave me your jacket.

HONEY. But I'll be cold.

LIBBY. Oh, alright. Hurry.

(**HONEY** *exits.*)

LIBBY. Hi.

ROSE. Hi.

LIBBY. I'm Libby.

ROSE. I'm Rose. We met Saturday night.

LIBBY. I remember. You seem really familiar. Have we met before?

ROSE. I think I have once of those faces. Everyone says that.

LIBBY. That's funny. Listen, let me give you some advice. Steer clear of Badger for a while. You don't want Gretchen Black to hate you.

ROSE. Why should I care?

LIBBY. Gretchen is...well, she's sort of...evil.

ROSE. Maybe she's just misunderstood.

LIBBY. No. Honey is misunderstood. Gretchen is evil.

ROSE. I'm not afraid of her.

LIBBY. I know Badger's cute and all, but he's not worth it. He's...confused.

ROSE. Who isn't? Aren't you?

LIBBY. No, I don't have time to be confused. I have a best friend to obey, a boyfriend to suck off, an after school job and a shitload of homework. My God, I miss Hoyt. I have to go.

ROSE. Who's Hoyt?

LIBBY. What? Nobody. Forget it.

ROSE. Is there a drama club at this school?

LIBBY. There is. Why?

ROSE. I want to join.

LIBBY. You are determined to be persecuted here, aren't you?

ROSE. Yes.

LIBBY. That's wonderful. I'm going that way now. Come on, I'll take you.

(*LIGHTS DOWN in the BATHROOM.*)

(*LIGHTS UP in the AUDITORIUM after school.* **LAUREL** *is trying to start the meeting. Everyone is preoccupied.*)

LAUREL. Hello people. I'm calling this Season Planning meeting to order now. I'll start by taking roll. Hoyt?

(**HOYT** *doesn't answer.*)

LAUREL. Hoyt? Is Hoyt present?

DONNIE. He's right in front of you.

LAUREL. Is your name Hoyt?

RONNIE. No, his name's Donnie.

DONNIE. And this is Ronnie.

LAUREL. Hoyt!!

(**HOYT** *puts down his book with a dreamy sigh.*)

HOYT. Yes, Your Majesty?

LAUREL. Are you here?

HOYT. In what sense?

LAUREL. Are you present? At this meeting? Are you physically in the room?

(**HOYT** *looks around, confused.*)

HOYT. Can't you see me in the room?

LAUREL. No Hoyt, I can't. Sometimes your brilliance shines so bright all I see is a blinding white pulse coming from your direction. So if you wouldn't mind indulging me...

HOYT. Whatever you desire, Your Royal Highness.

LAUREL. And I think you've made your point with the epithets.

HOYT. Oh, but there are so many more to choose from.

RONNIE. Your Eminence.

DONNIE. Your Excellency.

HOYT. Reverend Mother.

LAUREL. He's my cousin. I didn't have a choice.

HOYT. Ah, the trappings of the landed gentry.

LAUREL. I didn't exactly see explosives strapped to your chest, Tolstoy, so shut the fuck up.

HOYT. Laurel, something occurred to me today during my free period and I would like to share it with the group.

LAUREL. This is roll call. Announcements come later.

HOYT. Our teachers hate us. They don't want us to learn. They don't want us to be here. They just want us to die. (*beat*) I stumbled upon this revelation quite by accident when yesterday, *out of curiosity,* I asked Mr. Cornelius to prove that centrifugal force doesn't actually exist. He couldn't do it. He could open up a book and point to an equation. But he couldn't stop my book bag from hitting Costen Lyons' shin when I

spun it by its strap. He could put me in detention for a
month. But he couldn't keep Costen's shin from turning black and blue.

LAUREL. Are you trying to tell us you have detention for a
month?

HOYT. What I'm trying to tell you is – this is bullshit – this
whole school thing. Which leads me to my next point.
Love is a disease, like syphilis, that firstly ravages the
body and ultimately destroys the mind. And we're all
gonna get it.

LAUREL. Jesus Hoyt, that's not even something I would say.

DONNIE. Not to mention, an absolute nonsequitur.

HOYT. I'm proving a paradigmatic point here, Donnie. The
world is one big lie because everyone over twenty is
deranged.

LAUREL. Hoyt, just because Libby broke up with you –

HOYT. This has nothing to do with Libby. Love is a disease.
It's chemical. They've proven it. It's just hormones.
That stimulate euphoria. In this one tiny section of
the brain. The same tiny section that lights up when
people snort coke. People get close enough. They
like each other's smell. They fuck. The hormones get
released. The receptors pick them up, euphoria ensues
and you're literally addicted to love. But because the
human condition is intrinsically disappointing, everyone eventually bores everyone else to tears. Soon, we
can't stand each other in the moments we aren't fucking. It occurs to us that we miss reading. So we break
up. And enter withdrawal. Which hurts. Because it's
chemical. Some people take drugs, some people over-
eat, but to keep the pain at bay, the poet decides to
write about love. So we've got all these towering liter-
ary achievements composed during a state of chemical
withdrawal. The truth is, he doesn't actually remember love. He can barely remember to eat. But he has
to write something, so he makes shit up. Preposterous
things like love…completed him or made him a better

HOYT. *(cont.)* man. He invents women with lips as red as roses and hearts as pure as snow. *(beat)* There are no women like that. He's lying. And thus he perpetuates the ultimate cosmic joke. That love makes life worth living. Which we all read. And believe. Because we're children and stupid. And then we grow up and fall into the exact same trap. And spend the remainder of our lives in perpetual rehab with the rest of humanity.

(LAUREL starts to pack up her things.)

HOYT. Where are you going?

LAUREL. I quit.

HOYT. I know it's hard to hear, Laurel.

LAUREL. What is hard about this situation Hoyt, is that this is drama club. We're supposed to be rehearsing a play. Which we don't have anyone to cast in. Because everyone keeps quitting. Because you keep scaring them off.

HOYT. I would actually argue it's the human condition that keeps scaring everyone off.

DONNIE. You're both wrong. It's Roy. What happened to Roy. People think it may be catching.

RONNIE. Donnie and I have been getting a lot of weird looks lately.

DONNIE. Like we're...

RONNIE. You know...

DONNIE. Which is just stupid...

RONNIE. 'cause we love...

DONNIE. You know...

RONNIE. Tits...

DONNIE. Boobs.

RONNIE. Breasts.

DONNIE. Anything lactiferous.

RONNIE. We love milk.

DONNIE. Does a body good.

RONNIE. So we bought.

DONNIE. These matching belt buckles.

RONNIE. Confederate flags.

DONNIE. Just so people would think...

RONNIE. We're good 'ole boys...

DONNIE. And leave us alone.

RONNIE. And besides they're shiny.

DONNIE. And besides they hold our jeans up.

RONNIE. So our asses look tight. Tight as...

DONNIE. Boobs.

RONNIE. Which we like –

DONNIE. Love.

    (silence)

LAUREL. Right, well, would you look at the time? If I'm late to Cotillion one more time, my mother will disown me.

HOYT. What about the play?

LAUREL. You're depressed, Hoyt. I don't know how to help you anymore.

HOYT. I'm not depressed. I'm infected. You'd rather spend your afternoon curtseying to racists and homophobes?

LAUREL. They may be racists and homophobes but at least they're dancing.

DONNIE. Ronnie and I have to quit too.

HOYT. What? Why?

DONNIE. We're gonna take up rodeo instead.

RONNIE. Y'all don't ever do anything here.

DONNIE. We just want to be onstage.

RONNIE. See our name in lights.

DONNIE. We don't really like theatre.

RONNIE. But what else do you do when you're not popular in high school?

DONNIE. We thought we had no choice.

RONNIE. Until we discovered rodeo.

DONNIE. They've got beer and they've got hoofing.

RONNIE. And at halftime, they've got a short-short contest.

DONNIE. And you only got to stay on for eight seconds.

RONNIE. How hard could it be?

LAUREL. Alright boys, come on. I'll drive you home. Goodbye Hoyt.

(**HOYT** *will not answer. He lies down with a book over his head.*)

Mature, Hoyt. Real mature.

(**DONNIE, RONNIE** *and* **LAUREL** *exit.* **HOYT** *doesn't move. A moment later,* **LIBBY** *and* **ROSE** *appear, silhouetted in the doorway.*)

LIBBY. This is where they rehearse. Oh wow, I'd forgotten how dark it gets in here. Hello?

(**HOYT** *raises his head.*)

I guess they aren't here now, Rose. Maybe they've changed the meeting time.

(**HOYT** *lays his head back down on the floor.*)

HOYT. What can I do for you Libby?

LIBBY. Hoyt?

(No response.)

LIBBY. *(searching for Hoyt in the darkness)* Hoyt? I can't…I can't…

HOYT. Oh Hoyt, I can't – I can't – I mean, I want to but it hurts and oh, wait, isn't that Costen Lyons smiling at me?

LIBBY. Hoyt, stop it. There's someone here with me.

HOYT. Costen?

LIBBY. Don't be ridiculous, no.

HOYT. Someone new then? I hope you're rich man, because otherwise, you will be sorely, *sorely* disappointed by next period.

LIBBY. You're scum Hoyt.

HOYT. And you, my dear, are a carpetbagger.

ROSE. Come on, Libby, you don't need this. Let's go down to the Snack Shack and get a milkshake or something.

(HOYT sits up abruptly.)

HOYT. Who've you got there Libby?

LIBBY. Fine, I'm really sorry about this. He's probably stoned. He's always stoned.

HOYT. I'm never stoned. I'm simply eighteen, too smart for my own good, and therefore, extraordinarily unhappy. Who is that?

LIBBY. *(wearily)* Hoyt, this is Rose. She's new. Rose, Hoyt, Hoyt, Rose.

(ROSE steps into the light. Because they were best friends, HOYT immediately recognizes ROY.)

ROSE. It's a pleasure to meet you. I'm interested in joining your club.

HOYT. You've got to be fucking kidding me.

ROSE. My name is Rose White. I just moved into town.

HOYT. What's the matter with your face?

ROSE. You don't like it?

HOYT. You wear too much makeup.

LIBBY. Hoyt! You're being rude.

HOYT. Libby, you're no longer my girlfriend. I don't have to be polite around you anymore. I don't have to pretend to like your friends. I can just be myself. I'm free.

LIBBY. Come on Rose. That milkshake sounds really good.

HOYT. Does Costen hold your hair back while you puke? *(beat)*. Just wondering.

ROSE. When did you two break up?

LIBBY. Who remembers? Ages ago. We barely dated.

HOYT. We dated for two years! We broke up almost four months ago and I know that, not because I EVER cared about you, but because you dumped me a week after Roy disappeared and today is the four month anniversary of his disappearance.

ROSE. Who's Roy?

HOYT. Who indeed?

LIBBY. Roy was Hoyt's best friend. He disappeared.

ROSE. Where did he go?

HOYT. Who cares? He was a nut. He probably offed himself or something.

LIBBY. Hoyt!

HOYT. The kid was totally self-destructive.

LIBBY. He was not.

HOYT. He was never happy unless he was putting himself in danger. When we were kids, he used to run through fires like other kids ran through sprinklers.

LIBBY. He might be dead for all you know. Why are you saying such horrible things about him?

HOYT. He's not dead. He's fine.

LIBBY. You don't know that.

HOYT. I think I do. What do you think, Rose?

LIBBY. How would she know?

ROSE. *(changing the subject)* So I've heard you've written a marvelous play.

*(Pause. **HOYT** makes a decision here to play along. For the rest of the scene, he is much more animated, almost gleeful.)*

HOYT. You've heard wrong. I've written a sophomoric, mostly average, sometimes painful, totally unproducible play.

ROSE. Why unproducible?

HOYT. Well, for starters, nobody will act in it.

ROSE. That's why I'm here. I want to act in it.

HOYT. That's because you're new and you have no idea what an asshole I am to work with. You'll find out in about two seconds and then you'll quit with the rest of the Drama Club.

LIBBY. What? The whole Drama Club quit?

HOYT. Why sound so surprised Libby? You were the first one to leave, after all.

LIBBY. Yeah, but I loved the club. I left because —

HOYT. You wanted to be popular. Well, it looks like you got your wish. Look how popular you've become. You're popular enough to start trends.

LIBBY. Where's Laurel?

HOYT. She went to Cotillion.

ROSE. Laurel went to Cotillion?

LIBBY. Do you know Laurel?

ROSE. I met her briefly at Homecoming. She really didn't strike me as a Cotillion kind of girl.

LIBBY. She's not. Jesus, Hoyt, what did you do to drive Laurel to Cotillion?

HOYT. I didn't drive her to Cotillion. The human condition drove her to Cotillion.

ROSE. Listen lovelies, if Libby can start a trend, she can reverse it. Hoyt, what if I told you we could have a cast ready to rehearse by tomorrow afternoon?

HOYT. Impossible.

ROSE. Libby and I will start making flyers tonight and post them all over school. What's your play called?

HOYT. Syphilitic Love.

ROSE. Good title. How many characters?

HOYT. Just a guy and a girl.

ROSE. Done.

HOYT. I don't think so.

ROSE. Do you want to see this play produced or not?

HOYT. Of course I want to see it produced. But I've acclimatized myself to the fact that it isn't likely.

LIBBY. Acclimatized?

HOYT. It's a vocab word this week.

LIBBY. I don't think you're using it right.

HOYT. Fuck off. The main guy needs to be hot, okay? Really hot or the play won't work. And hot guys NEVER DO THEATRE.

(The door swings open. Enter **BADGER.** *)*

BADGER. Hi? Is Rose here? Oh there you are. Hey baby.

ROSE. Hey Badger. I thought you had football practice.

BADGER. I quit the team.

ROSE. Why?

BADGER. I wanted to keep my afternoons free to spend time with you. What are you doing here?

ROSE. I'm in the Drama Club now. Want to join?

BADGER. Why not? Where do I sign?

(The door swings open again. This time, it's **GRETCHEN**.*)*

GRETCHEN. Libby! Is Libby Sunday in here?

HOYT. This used to be such a happy place.

GRETCHEN. Libby, I know you're in here. I can smell your fear.

*(***GRETCHEN*** *slams the door and comes storming into the room.)*

GRETCHEN. I thought it might interest you to know one of your former friends is down at the Snack Shack, bleeding through a neon green coat. Oh hello Badger. Rose. I guess this is the place all the cool kids hang out for seventh period now.

LIBBY. Honey is bleeding? I sent her to give you last night's chemistry assignment. What did you do to her?

GRETCHEN. I didn't do anything to her. I had Costen snap her bra strap so hard it cut the skin.

LIBBY. Why?

GRETCHEN. She tried to talk to me.

HOYT. Get out. Get out of the auditorium.

GRETCHEN. I beg your pardon. This is not your auditorium. This is school property.

HOYT. Did you see that sign on the door? The one that says "no animals?" Get out.

GRETCHEN. Fine. I'll leave you moles to this hovel. I'm not afraid to walk in the sun. I'm gorgeous. Come on Badger, we're leaving.

*(***BADGER*** *is staring at* **ROSE** *dreamily and doesn't respond.)*

GRETCHEN. Badger!

BADGER. *(annoyed)* What?

GRETCHEN. Are you coming?

BADGER. Where?

GRETCHEN. Don't you have football practice?

BADGER. I quit.

GRETCHEN. You did what?

BADGER. I'm in the Drama Club now.

GRETCHEN. *(to* **ROSE***)* You will not get away with this, you pasty little ho.

ROSE. You know Gretchen, you have quite the dramatic streak yourself. Perhaps you would like to join us.

GRETCHEN. We all have secrets, Rose. Poison hiding in our hearts. I will find yours. And I will make it flow out every pore of your sickly skin.

(turning to **HOYT***)*

GRETCHEN. Alright asshole, what's my part?

(pause)

ROSE. Give her a script, Hoyt.

HOYT. Why not? The scripts are in the green room. Give them a once over and meet back here in ten.

GRETCHEN. Libby? Is he speaking English?

BADGER. I don't know of any green rooms.

LIBBY. Come with me. I'll show you. This is turning out to be a really weird day.

BADGER. I'm really happy.

GRETCHEN. No you're not Badger, shut up.

(Exit **LIBBY**, **BADGER** *and* **GRETCHEN**. *Leaving* **HOYT** *alone with* **ROSE**.*)*

HOYT. You should be institutionalized.

ROSE. I was. Didn't help.

HOYT. I thought your father said he'd skin you alive if you ever set foot in this county again.

ROSE. My father is dead. My stepfather said he'd skin me alive if I ever showed *my face* in this county again.

HOYT. Then what do you think you're –

ROSE. Does this look like my face to you?

HOYT. You'll get caught.

ROSE. I know. But I love him. So I don't have a choice.

HOYT. He's so not worth it.

ROSE. This coming from the man who has his nuts in a knot over Libby Sunday.

HOYT. She's really hot.

ROSE. She's anorexic.

(beat)

HOYT. I never expected to see you again.

ROSE. I wasn't worried. I figured, after high school, you'd find me or I'd find you.

HOYT. After high school? What do you mean?

ROSE. Hoyt, I'm gonna let you in on a little secret you're not supposed to know. High school? Ends. People graduate every year.

HOYT. That's what they say. But they make things up. It's a subjugation tactic. Because if everyone knew the truth – there'd be revolution.

ROSE. What's the truth?

HOYT. The truth is – after graduation we'll just be shuffled around – redistributed – and we'll have to begin high school again somewhere else.

ROSE. Hoyt. Lay off the pot.

(Enter LIBBY, holding a script.)

LIBBY. Hoyt, what the fuck is this?

(LIGHTS down.)

(LIGHTS UP. ROSE and BADGER on stage, scripts in hand, rehearsing the final scene of the play.)

BADGER. In the end, I guess I should thank you, Lily.

ROSE. Thank me Harry? But why?

BADGER. If you hadn't dumped me for the captain of the football team, I would have never had the motivation to write the greatest novel of our time – inspiring the *New York Times* to anoint me, and I quote, "Hemingway Reincarnate."

ROSE. I don't know what to say.

BADGER. Say "you're welcome," Lily.

ROSE. You're welcome Lily.

BADGER. My God, could I have ever loved one so stupid? But then again, I was young and incarcerated in a small southern private school. Our choices were to love or die.

ROSE. I'm glad you chose love, Harry.

BADGER. I'm not Lily. If I hadn't, I would have died, but at least I would have died an educated person. Because of you, all I've retained from high school is how to hurt and how to hate.

ROSE. I still don't know what to say, Harry.

BADGER. Don't say anything darling, just kiss me once before I go off to accept my Pulitzer and you go back to the trailer park.

ROSE. If only I hadn't been so stupid, Harry.

BADGER. It's too late, darling. It's too late.

(**ROSE** *and* **BADGER** *kiss. Suddenly, they both open their eyes and look at each other, surprised. A moment of recognition.*)

BADGER. I can't.

ROSE. Badger. Don't be frightened.

(**ROSE** *reaches for* **BADGER.** *He slaps her hand away.*)

BADGER. I'm sorry – I can't. I have to go. I'm late to football practice.

ROSE. Badger wait!

BADGER. Coach is gonna kill me. I have to go.

(**HOYT** *jumps on stage.* **LIBBY** *and* **GRETCHEN** *enter from the wings.*)

HOYT. Badger, man, you were great.

BADGER. I have to go.

,HOYT. But, I've got to give you some notes.

BADGER. I have to go. I'm not part of this club. I'm on a different team.

(The door swings open and **COSTEN** *enters.)*

COSTEN. Badger Biers!

BADGER. Costen, man, am I ever glad to see you. I've never been happier to see anyone in my entire –

*(***BADGER*** moves to embrace* **COSTEN.** **COSTEN** *shoves him away violently.)*

COSTEN. You little faggot. I can't believe I fucking found you here. You missed practice this afternoon.

BADGER. I'm so sorry, man.

COSTEN. I started at quarterback instead of you.

BADGER. That's great, man. You've wanted to start forever. How did it go?

COSTEN. Badly.

BADGER. Shit.

COSTEN. Coach sent me to find you and beg you to come back to the team. He said, and I quote, "Tell him, 'A pussy is a pussy is a pussy, but a championship ring is like having a second cock.'"

BADGER. He said that? Coach did?

COSTEN. Sure did.

BADGER. That's beautiful.

COSTEN. I know. He also said the only way I'd get to participate in practice tomorrow, after my performance today, was if I brought you with me. If I'm kicked off the team, you know how my father will react.

BADGER. He'll fire someone.

COSTEN. Hospital bills start adding up, Badge. So what do you say?

BADGER. I say, I'm coming with you to practice tomorrow.

GRETCHEN. Praise Jesus.

ROSE. Badger, what about…Hoyt's play?

HOYT. It's okay. Let him go.

ROSE. No. Badger, you made me a promise.

COSTEN. New girl. He's with Jesus now. You can't hurt him anymore.

BADGER. I said I'd try. It's too hard.

ROSE. You call that a try?

BADGER. I have tried in my mind. Night after night after night. It's too hard.

(**ROSE** *tries to embrace* **BADGER.** *He shoves her.*)

BADGER. Leave me alone.

(**BADGER** *leaves.*)

(**COSTEN** *follows* **GRETCHEN** *out.*)

(**HOYT, LIBBY** *and* **ROSE** *remain on stage.*)

ROSE. Hoyt, can I crash with you for a few days?

LIBBY. Is there something going on between you two?

ROSE. Damn it, Libby. How stupid are you?

LIBBY. Not stupid at all. I got a scholarship to a really, REALLY good college.

ROSE. He's been in love with you since the second grade. He will love you until he dies. Costen Lyons is a Nazi. What is the matter with you?

HOYT. Alright, that's enough.

LIBBY. Um, you just got here. What do you know?

ROSE. Nothing. Apparently, I know nothing. I'm sorry. I'm going to wash my face.

LIBBY. Do you want me to come with you?

ROSE. No.

LIBBY. You don't understand. In this town, the mirrors-have minds of their own.

ROSE. (*smiling sadly*) They don't scare me. I know what I'm hiding.

(**ROSE** *exits.*)

LIBBY. Is she crazy?

HOYT. I think she's just unhappy.

(LIBBY *and* HOYT *look at each other.*)

LIBBY. So.

HOYT. So.

LIBBY. So…is that true?

HOYT. No.

LIBBY. Good. Because I'm with Costen now.

HOYT. Whom you absolutely deserve.

LIBBY. Fuck you.

HOYT. Never again, thank God. What a nightmare that was.

LIBBY. See, this is exactly why we broke up. You were totally unsupportive.

HOYT. Costen, on the other hand, is blessed with the patience and serenity of a eunuch.

LIBBY. At least he doesn't pretend to love me. At least I know all he wants from me is a fuck.

HOYT. I did love you. I also wanted to sleep with you. What do you want from me? I'm eighteen and you're really hot.

(pause)

LIBBY. You and Laurel were always so cynical. We never got to *do* anything. We just sat around and made fun of other people for doing things. Even Roy got sick of it all. He told me, before he disappeared, that he was going to quit drama club and manage the football team.

HOYT. He did not.

LIBBY. He did. I never told you because you already seemed to be in so much pain. But it's true. We were both just so tired of hating everyone we knew.

HOYT. I never hated you.

LIBBY. That's because we were having sex. As soon as we stopped, you would have hated me too.

(beat)

HOYT. You can't honestly believe that.

LIBBY. I can honestly believe whatever I want, Hoyt. You have no idea how powerful I actually am. I can stay up for three days straight on nothing but whipped cream, coffee and sugar-free jello. Do you know how many calories that is, Hoyt? I do. I know how many calories you consume by licking the back of a stamp. I also know how the French revolution got so out of control and why centrifugal force doesn't actually exist. I know everyone's name in this school, what their current GPA is and what they eat for lunch each day. And I think about food almost every moment of every day so can you imagine how much more I would know if I never had to eat again? No, of course you can't. Because you're not nearly as smart as me.

HOYT. You promised me you were going to get help. You promised me you were going to try and get better.

LIBBY. I don't have time to get help, asshole! This is why I'm with Costen now. He likes me just the way I am. He's not trying to ferry me off to the loony bin.

HOYT. Jesus Christ, Libby, I wanted you to go to therapy. That's all.

LIBBY. I'm fine.

HOYT. No, you're not.

LIBBY. What do you care?

HOYT. I love you.

LIBBY. Bullshit.

HOYT. I swear it's true.

LIBBY. Then you're stupid.

HOYT. I don't care. Listen, my mother made peach cream and biscuits this morning. Let's go pack a picnic and watch the sunset over Moonlight lake.

LIBBY. I'm not hungry.

HOYT. *(desperately)* Libby.

LIBBY. *(a challenge)* Hoyt.

HOYT. Guys like curves. How many times do I have to tell you that?

LIBBY. I am not doing this for you or Costen or any guy.

HOYT. Then why – sweetheart – why are you –

LIBBY. I like being light, Hoyt. I want to be lighter. I want to be so light I could step into the air if I were ever in trouble and fly away.

(HOYT *and* LIBBY *stare at each other.*)

(*Enter* LAUREL.)

LAUREL. Hoyt! I need to talk to you. What is Libby doing here? I thought she quit.

HOYT. It's a long story. What's going on? You want to join the club again? Welcome back. I forgive you.

LAUREL. Libby, can you leave us alone?

LIBBY. I don't think so. No.

LAUREL. Why not?

LIBBY. You wouldn't share your joint at Homecoming.

LAUREL. Fine, be that way. I don't care anymore. I just want to say it. Hoyt, I love you. I know you don't love me. I can't help it. Maybe it's your smell. But I can't take it anymore. It's ruining my life. I wake up in the mornings in a cold sweat. I have no appetite. I can't concentrate. I am totally unproductive. There are millions of mal-nourished, HIV positive orphans in Africa. Millions! And I can do nothing but lie in my bed for hours and stare at the ceiling. I've tried everything I can think of. I stand in front of the bathroom mirror every morning. I tell myself you are self-absorbed and whiny and immature and you only like social-climbing airheads.

LIBBY. Hey!

LAUREL. I tell myself that you kick puppies for fun and nothing works. I still feel like I'm having a heart attack every time you speak to me.

HOYT. You are really good at hiding that.

LAUREL. I know. But I can't take it anymore. I have to get into college. So I need to hear from you, from your own lips, that you and I will never be together. I need you to be a total asshole, so I can hate you. And I need you to do it now because I have to take the SATs in the morning.

(HOYT *looks from* LAUREL *to* LIBBY *and back again.*)

LIBBY. A picnic sounds nice, Hoyt.

HOYT. Libby and I were just about to take a picnic to Moonlight Lake. Want to come?

(*Beat.* LAUREL *just stares at him.*)

HOYT. You don't need me. She needs me.

LAUREL. She's using you.

LIBBY. You get to be a debutante. Cry me a river.

LAUREL. (*a single shot*) You look fat.

(HOYT *gets up abruptly.*)

HOYT. I'm going somewhere else. To read.

LIBBY. I'll come with you.

LAUREL. I'm leaving too.

HOYT. I'm leaving first. Nobody moves.

(HOYT *sprints to the door.* LAUREL *and* LIBBY *stare at each other. Lights down.*)

(*Lights rise in the* BOYS LOCKER ROOM. BADGER *is standing in front of the mirror with his eyes closed and his football helmet in his hand. He is concentrating.*)

BADGER. Maggot, maggots, maggots.

(ROSE *enters the bathroom silently and stands behind him facing the mirror.*)

BADGER. One, two, three.

(BADGER *opens his eyes and sees the reflection of* ROSE *in the mirror behind him.*)

BADGER. Dammit.

ROSE. I'll tell you a story. About a prince. He was beautiful. With hair as golden as the sun and eyes the color of moonlight on a country lake. He was trapped inside a glass casket. He was pretending to be asleep. Because

ROSE. *(cont.)* it was easier. If they thought he was asleep,
   they'd leave him alone. At least he could dream. But
   one night, he had been in the glass casket so long,
   so frightfully still, he dreamt he was dead. When he
   tried to open his eyes, he couldn't. The people outside
   were very sad. They assumed he had passed on. But
   they rejoiced because he was already in a casket. And
   so they left him there. For the rest of his life. Not dead
   exactly, but he sure as fuck wasn't living.

   (BADGER turns around.)

BADGER. Subtle, Roy.

   *(ROSE removes her wig and will heretofore be known as
   ROY.)*

ROY. Well, you can be a bit dense.

BADGER. If Costen finds you in here, he'll beat the shit out
   of you.

ROY. You'll protect me.

BADGER. No, I won't. I can't.

ROY. No, I know. I was being ironic.

   (ROY starts to disrobe.)

BADGER. What are you doing?

ROY. If Costen is gonna pummel me, I don't want to get
   blood all over my dress. I love this dress. I want to wear
   it again.

BADGER. Would you please keep your clothes on?

ROY. What's the matter? Afraid you won't be able to control yourself?

BADGER. Me? What about you? You're the one who's –

ROY. Wearing a dress? *(He steps out of his dress.)* Not anymore.

BADGER. Are those my boxers?

ROY. They might be.

BADGER. Look, you have to go.

ROY. Come with me.

BADGER. I can't.

ROY. You CAN leave. Nobody is going to stop you. The universe is expanding, even as we speak. It's making room for you and me. You stay here, you'll marry my sister and I guarantee you, you'll kill yourself before your thirtieth birthday. You won't even know you're doing it. You'll put a pillow over your face one night to block out her smell and you'll forget to take it off. But come with me now and they'll be nothing but mountains to climb and oceans to sail and cities to conquer. And love. Years and years of love.

BADGER. You look good, Roy. Really, really good.

ROY. So do you.

BADGER. You're going to have a wonderful life, I can tell. You'll die a happy man.

ROY. Badger –

BADGER. My mother is going to die.

ROY. How is she?

BADGER. Still smoking. She's in a lot of pain now. She's trying to get to heaven as quickly as possible.

ROY. I hope she's not disappointed.

BADGER. Nobody is disappointed by heaven. Don't be an infidel.

ROY. If it's anything like my stepfather says, I'm going to be bored to tears.

BADGER. I wouldn't worry if I were you.

ROY. You don't think it sounds boring?

BADGER. I don't think you're going. *(beat)* I'm going.

ROY. Of course you will. In sixty years or so. Your mother would want you to live a life. A long and happy life.

BADGER. Yes, but I won't get there if I keep doing things like…this.

(**BADGER** *indicates himself and* **ROY.**)

ROY. You don't know that.

BADGER. I do know that. Everyone knows that. You've just chosen to forget it and that's fine for you. It's your decision. You've still got a mother and you hate her anyway. But it's different for me. My mother is saint and Jesus is taking her early because they need her in heaven. She ain't even gonna see me graduate. Or marry. Or meet her grandchildren. I'll be damned before I desecrate her memory by sodomizing like a dog on earth while she's up in heaven trying to teach the angels *how to be good.*

ROY. I love you Badger Biers. I think you love me too.

BADGER. It doesn't matter.

ROY. You deserve to be happy, don't you?

BADGER. Happy? What kind of a world do you live in? That's a child's question. I'm not even gonna dignify it with an answer. When you become a man – if you ever become a man – you'll be able to answer it yourself.

(**BADGER** *starts to exit.*)

ROY. I'm not leaving without you.

BADGER. *(tired)* Yes, you are.

ROY. But I came back to save you.

BADGER. From who?

ROY. My stepfather…Gretchen…all of them!

BADGER. Your stepfather is just an old fool on a pulpit and your sister just needs someone to be kind. I'll be fine, Roy. This is where I belong.

(**BADGER** *hesitates, then kisses* **ROY.**)

Lord Jesus, you have to go.

(**BADGER** *looks at himself in the mirror.*)

BADGER. Hey, will you look at that?

ROY. What?

BADGER. He's gone.

ROY. Who?

(**BADGER** *smiles at* **ROY** *in the mirror.*)

BADGER. My locker is number 27 if you need some clothes. Please – don't follow me.

*(**BADGER** exits.)*

*(**ROY** is left alone, staring at himself in the mirror. A moment later, **GRETCHEN** enters.)*

GRETCHEN. Badger? *(She sees **ROY** and immediately puts it all together.)* Roy. You came back.

ROY. Hiya Gretch.

GRETCHEN. How's school?

ROY. It sucks. How are Mom and Dad?

GRETCHEN. Evil. *(beat)* I've been meaning to write to you. To see if you needed anything. Do you need anything?

*(**ROY** stares at her.)*

Did you have a nice summer?

*(**ROY** doesn't answer.)*

GRETCHEN. Mom says she's been sending you money. Is she sending enough? I could tell her you need more.

(No response.)

GRETCHEN. She says the school is nice. Is it nice?

ROY. It's nice.

GRETCHEN. You must be very happy.

ROY. Why would I be happy?

GRETCHEN. If the school is nice –

ROY. Everyone I love is here.

GRETCHEN. There must be people there that you could love.

ROY. If you think that, you don't understand love at all.

GRETCHEN. Oh, but of course, you do.

ROY. I've tasted it.

GRETCHEN. No, Roy, you've tasted sex. It's not the same thing. True love is about honor and tradition and decency. True love can only exist between two people, preferably of similar heritage, who make a

GRETCHEN. *(cont.)* commitment to each other and to their community to live happily ever after. How can you understand love? You don't even understand decency.

ROY. You're a hick Gretchen. I'm sorry if my sexual orientation confuses you –

GRETCHEN. I don't give a fuck about your sexual orientation. You seduced my boyfriend. Your sister's boyfriend. That is not *decent*. That is not *courteous*. That is not SOUTHERN.

    (pause)

ROY. He doesn't love you.

GRETCHEN. Do you?

ROY. You betrayed me.

GRETCHEN. You betrayed me first.

ROY. You didn't tell them who – who you found me with. You never told them it was Badger.

GRETCHEN. No.

ROY. They never asked?

GRETCHEN. No.

ROY. Badger never said anything? When I left, did he – did you ever – do you ever speak of me?

GRETCHEN. No.

ROY. Nothing has changed. I've just disappeared.

GRETCHEN. The mirrors are cursed. Other than that, it's exactly the same.

ROY. Everybody keeps saying that. What the hell does that mean?

GRETCHEN. Remember that thing you used to do when we were kids? That trick you made up to make me feel pretty?

ROY. Yes.

GRETCHEN. It doesn't work anymore.

ROY. Why not?

GRETCHEN. Try it. Please.

ROY. Will you do it with me?

    (GRETCHEN nods.)

(**GRETCHEN** *and* **ROY** *both turn to face the mirror. They close their eyes.*)

ROY. Mirror, mirror.

GRETCHEN. Mirror, mirror.

ROY. On the wall.

GRETCHEN. On the wall.

ROY. Who's the fairest.

GRETCHEN. Who's the fairest.

ROY. Of them all?

GRETCHEN. Of them all.

(*They open their eyes at the same time.*)

GRETCHEN. What do you see?

ROY. I see you and me. What do you see?

GRETCHEN. I see you and – and someone else.

ROY. You.

GRETCHEN. No. It's someone else. Some kind of hideous witch.

ROY. Look at yourself. There's your golden hair. There's your freckled skin. You can't see that?

GRETCHEN. (*shaking her head*) That isn't me. The mirrors are cursed.

ROY. They are pieces of glass, Gretch. Reflective glass. Whatever you see – you've put it there. Close your eyes.

(**GRETCHEN** *closes her eyes.*)

There's nobody in the mirror but you and me. Now open your eyes.

(**GRETCHEN** *opens her eyes.*)

ROY. Who do you see?

GRETCHEN. You and her.

ROY. Close them.

(**GRETCHEN** *closes her eyes.*)

There's nobody in the mirror but you and me. Open your eyes. Who do you see?

(GRETCHEN *opens her eyes and looks at* ROY.)

GRETCHEN. I can make her go away. Do you have a cigarette?

ROY. No. Close your eyes.

(GRETCHEN *sighs, but does it.*)

There's nobody in the mirror but you and me. Open your eyes. What do you see?

(GRETCHEN *winces at the mirror.*)

GRETCHEN. *(quietly)* Her.

ROY. Look again. What do you see?

GRETCHEN. *(desperately)* Her.

ROY. Look again.

Look again.

Look again.

(*Beat. Brother and sister stare into the mirror, side by side.*)

ROY. Look again.

(ROY *snaps his fingers.*)

(*The MIRROR lifts up and flies away. The benches, the lockers, the basketball hoops – everything disappears. If the auditorium curtain is on stage at this point, it parts to reveal, behind it...*)

(*Moonlight Lake.*)

(HOYT *and* BADGER *are already there, tangled in the trees/catwalk, hanging mirrors.* LIBBY *is spreading a picnic basket on the ground. In the lake itself, a thousand white orbs are bobbing, pieces of a fractured moon.*)

HOYT. *(to* BADGER*)* How's your mom?

BADGER. She's better, thanks. How's your heart?

HOYT. It's not bad. Not bad at all. Hey, look who finally showed up. It's Gretchen and Roy. Where have you two been? You better hurry up and get some of my mama's biscuits and peach cream before Libby eats them all.

LIBBY. Hoyt, my therapist doesn't think you take my eating disorder seriously.

HOYT. Libby is falling in love with her therapist.

BADGER. I'm pretty sure she's in love with you dude.

GRETCHEN. Roy, what's happening?

LIBBY. Don't mind them, darling. They're just hanging mirrors in the trees. Come, sit with me.

GRETCHEN. Is this a dream?

ROY. A dream, a story, insanity, high school. It's hard to tell sometimes, isn't it?

(COSTEN *and* LAUREL *dance by. Back in their prom costumes.*)

COSTEN. *(to* LAUREL*)* So much depends
upon a red wheel barrow
glazed with rainwater
beside the white chicken.

LAUREL. William Carlos Williams

COSTEN. It's the only poem I know.

LAUREL. You need an education cousin.

HOYT. Okay, y'all. We're finished.

BADGER. Take a look.

(BADGER *and* HOYT *climb down from the trees. Everyone looks into Moonlight Lake.*)

GRETCHEN. I've never seen so many moons.

LAUREL. It's beautiful, isn't it?

GRETCHEN. Where do they end?

COSTEN. I don't think they do.

(*Silence. Everyone stares contentedly into the lake.*)

BADGER. Hey Roy? Have they got lakes this beautiful in the North?

ROY. Oh no, they can't do anything like this up North.

BADGER. Why not?

ROY. They're far too literal.

(*Everyone accepts this answer as perfectly understandable as the moons fade and the play ends.*)

End of Play

ABOUT THE PLAYWRIGHT

Sarah Treem's full-length plays include *Empty Sky, Against The Wall, Mirror, Mirror, A Feminine Ending, Human Voices* and *The How And The Why*, which will receive its world premiere at McCarter Theatre in January 2011, directed by Emily Mann. *A Feminine Ending* received its world premiere at Playwrights Horizons in Fall 2007, was subsequently produced at South Coast Repertory and Portland Center Stage in 2008, and is published by Samuel French. *Human Voices* was part of Manhattan Theater Club's Springboard's New Play Series and New York Stage & Film's Powerhouse Reading Season in 2007. Sarah has been in residence at The Sundance Institute and The Ojai Playwriting Conference. She has been commissioned by South Coast Repertory and Playwrights Horizons, and she is a current fellow at the Lark Playwrights' Workshop. Sarah is a Writer/Producer on the acclaimed HBO series, *In Treatment;* as well as the Mark Wahlberg produced HBO series *How To Make It In America.* She is currently adapting Samantha Peale's novel *The American Painter Emma Dial* for HBO with Philip Seymour Hoffman and Emily Ziff. She graduated from Yale University and the Yale School of Drama.

OTHER TITLES AVAILABLE FROM SAMUEL FRENCH

A FEMININE ENDING

Sarah Treem

Full Length, Dark Comedy / 3m, 2f / Various, Unit set

Amanda, twenty-five, wants to be a great composer. But at the moment, she's living in New York City and writing advertising jingles to pay the rent while her fiancé, Jack, pursues his singing career. So when Amanda's mother, Kim, calls one evening from New Hampshire and asks for her help with something she can't discuss over the phone, Amanda is only too happy to leave New York. Once home, Kim reveals that she's leaving Amanda's father and needs help packing. Amanda balks and ends up (gently) hitting the postman, who happens to be her first boyfriend. They spend the night together in an apple orchard, where Amanda tries to tell Billy how her life got sidetracked. It has something to do with being a young woman in a profession that only recognizes famous men. Billy acts like he might have the answer, but doesn't. Neither does Amanda's mother. Or, for that matter, her father. A Feminine Ending is a gentle, bittersweet comedy about a girl who knows what she wants but not quite how to get it. Her parents are getting divorced, her fiancée is almost famous, her first love reappears, and there's a lot of noise in her head but none of it is music. Until the end.

"*Ending*' is a promising beginning...the playwright has a sense of humor that brings to mind a budding Wendy Wasserstein and a liberated sense of form that evokes a junior Paula Vogel."
– *Los Angeles Times*

"Darkly comic. *Feminine Ending* has undeniable wit."
– *New York Post*

"Appealingly outlandish humor."
– *The New York Times*

"Courageous. The 90-minute piece swerves with nerve and naivete. Sarah Treem has a voice all her own."
– *Newsday*

SAMUELFRENCH.COM